Savvy Survival

…for women starting over alone later in life.

Caroline Sposto

Illustrations by Gina Sposto
Author Photo by Studio Norwood www.studionorwood.com

ISBN: 978-969-53-9246-1 (paperback)
ISBN: 978-969-53-9247-8 (hardback)

Table of Contents

I. Get Back on Your Feet

II. Step Into Your Power

III. Hit Your Stride

About the Author

Caroline *Zarlengo* Sposto is an award-winning writer and the founder of *Savvy Civility*. She holds a B.A. in English and an M.S. in Electronic Media and is a member of SAG-AFTRA and Equity. She's also a certified TESL Instructor, Life Coach, and Etiquette Consultant.

In 2014, when Caroline was in her early 50s, a series of unexpected events left her starting over from scratch on her own. She discovered that the talents she'd set aside during her 25-year marriage were crucial to her survival, success, and happiness. She wrote this book to encourage other women facing similar challenges to rediscover their strengths and rebuild their lives with flair, fearless independence, and fun! Caroline is also the proud mother of two grown daughters, who continue to be her greatest inspiration.

Disclaimer

This book is for self-discovery, motivational, and entertainment purposes only. It isn't intended to substitute for financial, legal, or medical advice.

Dedication

"Do what you feel is right in your heart—for you'll be criticized anyway."
—ELEANOR ROOSEVELT

To my inspiring daughters.

Acknowledgements

A special thanks to my close friends Sylvia Valentine, Shelby Elwood, Hal Harmon, and Gloria Stevens, who encouraged me throughout this project. My talented friend, Stephanie Norwood, who took my author photo. Author Richard Bausch, who gave me the confidence to write. Neena Laskowski and her team at Elite Authors who turned my Word document into an attractive book. And finally, my daughter, Gina Sposto, who created the cover art and interior illustrations.

Introduction

*"There will come a time when you believe everything
is finished. That will be the beginning."*
—Louis L'Amour

If you're suddenly single and starting over later in life, Ladies, you're not alone. Millions of us are out here, and our numbers are multiplying faster than dandelions in July.

I recently read a fascinating piece in the *New York Times*. Nowadays, folks 50-plus are more likely to be uncoupled than ever before. Divorced, widowed, separated—you name it—there are masses of us navigating the wild unknown, and most of us solo flyers are sassy, seasoned chicks!

In my early fifties, life whisked me from security to precariousness faster than you can say "house of cards." I'll spare you the details. Suffice it to say I felt like I was playing a game of *Who Can Betray Me Next?* and some of the people I trusted most—most notably my then-husband of 25 years—were trying to win first prize.

In classic "me" fashion, I raided libraries, bookstores, and the vast corners of the internet for motivation and advice. I found blogs, memoirs, self-help sagas, legal and financial guides, and divorce manuals. You throw it at me, and I've seen it. But nothing I read hit the mark—not even close.

Then, one day, about five years later, it dawned on me that I hadn't merely adapted to my "new normal." I had become a better version of myself—one with a heftier-than-ever dose of wisdom and resilience.

At that moment, I was in an airport, scrolling Facebook on my phone while waiting to board a flight. A meme with Toni Morrison's words popped up on my feed and smacked me right between the eyes: "If there's a book that you want to read, but it hasn't been written yet, then you must write it."

Moments later, still chewing on that thought, I was magically bumped to First Class. That little stroke of luck felt as if fate were nudging me. When we reached cruising altitude, I asked for a cup of jet-setting black coffee, cracked open my laptop, and started typing away. Years later, this book is finally finished, and Ladies, it's for you!

If you picked up this book for yourself, I don't need to tell you that the struggle you're facing didn't arrive in a tidy little package. It's a messy tangle of emotions and challenges, some of which seem as out of the blue and surreal as getting trampled by a herd of caffeinated llamas. Waving a white handkerchief won't save the day. But with a bit of moxie, you can learn to wrangle those llama dramas, have a blast doing it, and come out shining like a champ. Oh yes, you can!

At first, some challenges might seem as daunting as preparing a royal banquet with nothing more than a microwave and a toaster. In addition to the tangible adjustments, your emotions may feel like they've been hit by a freight train. But believe it or not, you're standing on the threshold of a new kind of freedom. And guess what? Once you cross that threshold, your life can be more exhilarating than ever before.

Long relationships may feel secure, but they're rarely perfect. Sleeping alone can feel empty, but so can sharing your bed with someone who kisses you on autopilot and hogs the covers. I know loss is hard, and grief takes its toll, but once you decide to adapt, the comeback you make can be nothing short of legendary.

Speaking of comebacks, let me tell you about a documentary I saw about a caterpillar turning into a butterfly. Did you know that little critter doesn't just sprout wings? She liquifies inside her chrysalis and grows into an almost magical creature using the same DNA. Metamorphosis, Ladies! It's an inside job!

Like that caterpillar, many of you may not yet have an inkling of your potential to transform. Well, it's time to wake up and believe in your own magic!

Whatever happened in your past, your future is a fresh canvas. Think of this book as your artist's palette. If you gradually pick and choose the hues of advice that speak to your soul, you'll end up with a new life, which is nothing less than a masterpiece as unique and beautiful as you are.

Of course, you'll have to do more than just read. Grab a pen and plenty of paper because the following pages are chockablock with self-reflection exercises. Dig into them like a tub of movie theater popcorn with extra butter. Remember, you're the captain of this journey, not a passenger. Take control and steer with purpose.

And hey! Speeding through this book like you're applying lipstick on a crowded train won't do nearly as much for you. Read the chapters in order. Do each exercise in a leisurely, self-reflective manner. Give yourself the gift of time because, as my uncle Leonard used to say, "If you want to accomplish something big, it's going to take a little longer."

Finally, don't hesitate to set this book aside and take a breather whenever you need it. Think of it as hitting the pause button on your favorite show—it'll be here when you're ready to dive back in. By the time you finish this process, I want you to be brimming with confidence and feeling like a million bucks.

All right, Ladies. You got this! Stick with me, and we'll paint the town red! Your comeback starts right here. Right now.

. . . Believe it or not, a lot of the best moments of your life haven't even happened yet . . .

Exercise 1: Document Your Starting Point

First Video Diary

Our brave little caterpillar didn't get to reflect on her butterfly glow-up. But your transformation? That's a whole different story.

Grab your camera, phone, or computer and make a short video of yourself before you embark on this journey. Do this alone with the intention of it being for your eyes only.

When you click "record," state the date and then answer these questions:

- If I knew I would succeed, what would I change about myself and my life?
- What will happen if I don't set new goals or make any changes?
- What are my biggest obstacles today?
- What are my biggest fears today?
- What are my biggest dreams today?

After you answer those questions, say whatever else you want to say.

At the end of this program, you'll record another video to see how far you've come.

Exercise 2: Positive Reflections

- Write down at least five things you've accomplished in life that you're proud of.
- Write down at least five strengths or qualities you admire in yourself.
- What is one positive thing you've done for yourself lately?
- Write down one simple thing you can do that will positively affect your life.
- Commit to doing that one simple thing as soon as possible.

I

Get Back on Your Feet

"If you're going through Hell, at least act like you own the place."
—UNKNOWN

Strange as it may sound, here's the best news I can give you:

Nobody is coming to your rescue. It's up to you to solve your problems and make things right. And that's more than okay. You're stronger than you realize, and this time, instead of being the damsel in distress, you get to be the badass babe in shining armor, slaying your own dragons and taking control!

What are you waiting for?

Grab up your jewel-encrusted sword, straighten your tiara, and keep reading . . .

1

Make Your Mindset Your BFF

"You cannot go back and change the beginning,
but you can start where you are and change the ending."
—C.S. LEWIS

Remember that childhood game, Chutes and Ladders? Starting over is a lot like that. Some days, you climb. Other days, you slide, and just when you think you've figured it out, loneliness sneaks in, making you feel as if you're stranded in a remote canyon trying to connect to Wi-Fi. But when that happens, you've got a choice: either stare at the "no signal" icon and stay stuck, or embrace your inner explorer, pull up your socks, and start climbing.

Now I know, early on, there may be days when the thought of getting out of bed seems as grueling as pushing a wheelbarrow full of bricks through quicksand. When that happens, focus on the basics: put your feet on the floor and get up—no matter what. Brush your teeth. Comb your hair. Take a shower. Make your bed. Eat something. Start small. The next time you wake up steeped in the same flavor of melancholy, push yourself a tiny bit further. If you feel deeply depressed for more than a week or two, reach out to a mental health professional for help. If you don't have health insurance, *Google* the free hotlines, join a support group, or see what counseling services your house of worship has to offer. Meanwhile, keep getting out of bed, getting cleaned up, and eating a bite every day . . . and stay with me through these pages.

Your mind is your personal universe. You have to live in it. Whether it seems like an opulent five-star resort or a shadowy haunted house depends largely on you. It's not always what we experience but what we focus on that makes all the difference. A positive attitude is more than a choice. It's the most valuable gift you can give yourself, especially right now. Never forget that you have the power to shape your experience. So do your best to see every glass as half full—preferably with *Dom Pérignon*!

Now, if positive thinking feels challenging, don't worry. It's not just you. Neuroscientists have discovered something fascinating: On an average day, the 86 billion neurons in that think tank between our ears churn out about 60,000 thoughts. Left to our own devices, a whopping 80% of those thoughts are negative, and 95% of them are on repeat—kind of like getting the chorus of that '70s pop song, "Seasons in the Sun," stuck in our heads.

Those gloomy thought stats can skyrocket during tough times. While we can't control every random thought, we can guide our active thinking. When you catch yourself spiraling into negativity, step back and curate your thoughts like a travel blogger curates their *Instagram* feed.

If you need a positive thought to get started, put your mind around this: Women today are living longer, staying more vibrant, seizing more opportunities, and diving into more adventures than our grandmothers ever dreamed possible. We get to choose our religion, goals, career, moral code, lifestyle, pronouns, hair color—you name it. How cool is that?

Now, I get it—I've been there. The end of a marriage or intimate partnership can make us feel like we're stuck in a never-ending bad reality show marathon. While we're tangled up in the mess of pain and confusion, it's easy to fall into a spin cycle of anger, regret, blame, self-pity, and worry. But it's up to us to press the reset button.

Whenever you catch yourself in a negative thought loop, hit that reset button—STAT! Stand tall in front of a mirror, look yourself in the eye, and say, "I've overcome plenty of challenges in my life. This is just another."

Or, as the philosopher once said, "When life hands you lemons, throw 'em back and demand some chocolate!"

We've all seen people respond to hard times by opting for a lifestyle of grief, but that's not for fabulous you! Our time on this earth is too short, and besides, nothing lasts forever—not even grief...or your Aunt Mildred's fruitcake.

Granted, our modern pendulum has swung so far in the "get over it" direction that mourning periods have gone the way of the telegram. Consequently, there'll be times you'll have to put on a brave face before you're ready. I have no doubt you'll rise to the occasion, but don't let that socially imposed mask turn into a pattern of denial. Bottling up your emotions is like squeezing into *Spanx*. It might smooth things out temporarily, but it doesn't address the real issues underneath. So, when you're alone or with someone you trust, let those feelings breathe, even if it means swearing like a sailor or ugly crying. Again, if you don't have a therapist or a support group, now is a good time to find one.

And remember, Ladies, your friends, relatives, coworkers, grown children, ex-husband, and strangers you meet in line at *Costco* are *not* your therapists. Please don't force them into that role. It may help to pour your heart out to a trusted friend or two once or twice at this stage, but professional counselors and support groups exist for a reason.

Whew! I'm glad we got that chapter out of the way!

Coming up next: Eight empowering pillars to help you navigate this journey with grace and strength. Stick around. You won't want to miss 'em. . .

2

Eight Empowering Pillars for Newly Independent Women

"Experience is the hardest teacher. It gives the
test before presenting the lesson."
—Oscar Wilde

1. **Don't hide behind your Wonder Woman cape.** When my life took a nosedive, I let my ego get in the way and pretended I was happier and more together than I really was. Believe me, living behind that facade only made things worse.

2. **Think like a camel.** When camels are loaded down, they don't ask for more to carry. We women tend to pile on obligations until we're on the verge of collapse. Take a page from the camel's playbook, and don't offer to do anything extra right now.

3. **Don't get caught up in the news.** We've been taught that staying well-informed is a responsibility—and to an extent, that's

true. However, constantly reading, hearing, and discussing depressing and harrowing stories won't do you any good right now. You're already dealing with enough. Glance at the headlines once a day and move on.

4. **Choose your coping mechanisms wisely.** Diving into a pitcher of martinis, a quarter pound of cocoa-dusted truffles, a clandestine sexual adventure, a bowl of marijuana, or a shopping spree may feel intoxicating, but in addition to being a mirage, escapes on this level tend to be a one-way ticket to Regretsville.

5. **Refuse delivery on the term "baggage."** We fabulous Ladies don't have baggage—we have rich experiences. In every epic tale, the heroine faces trials and tribulations. No one dares call her experiences "baggage." Be the heroine of your own story! Live like you're writing a bestseller, and make it an inspiring tale of triumph instead of a tear-jerker.

6. **Don't jump into major decisions.** Even if you don't feel vulnerable right now, you are, and there are vultures out there just waiting to swoop in and take advantage of newly single women. It might be that smooth-talking charmer who showers you with love one night and disappears into thin air the next morning or that investment opportunity that seems too good to be true. Now, I'm not saying you ought to go full-on conspiracy theorist and assume the worst about every little thing, but channel your inner skeptic and look before you leap.

7. **Have faith.** Despairing will get you nowhere. Believe that things will work out in the end because they will. I'm not talking about any particular religion. Your spiritual life is up to you. Here's a metaphor to illustrate what I mean: Think of the times you've walked into an unfamiliar building and

stepped into the elevator alone. You pushed a button, the doors closed, and you sensed you were moving, but all you could see were elevator doors. Unless you have a problem with elevators, you weren't fixating on the floor you left or worrying about what the floor you'd arrive on would look like. You weren't trying to steer the elevator. You knew the doors would open, and you'd step out exactly where you were supposed to be. Faith works the same way.

8. **Practice Gratitude.** Again, we're back to the "glass half full." Be thankful for what you have, the choices that await, and the opportunity to make a fresh start. You have the power to shape a brand new future that will suit you to a "T." How cool is that?

Of course, we'll explore some of these pillars in more detail later.

Exercise 3: Attitude Tune-Up

Only you can improve your attitude. The first step is taking an honest assessment of your current outlook.

Answer these questions honestly.
Have I recently caught myself . . .

> ... contradicting or interrupting people who were trying to help or encourage me?
> ... mentally preparing a list of reasons my life will never improve?
> ... indulging in thoughts centered around blame or revenge?
> ... feeling safer staying down since rising means I could fall again?

It's time to turn those insights into improvement. Look at your answers with a smile—no judgment here. Spot the negativity and show it the door. One universal measure of a great woman is how well she bears up under misfortune. *Dare to be great!*

3

Boundaries & Assertiveness

"A 'No' uttered from the deepest conviction is better than a 'Yes' merely uttered to please, or worse, avoid trouble."
—MAHATMA GANDHI

By this point in our lives, most of us have poured our hearts, souls, and a good chunk of our resources into our loved ones, friends, and communities. And let's be honest, a few of those folks wouldn't know gratitude if it smacked them in the head with a *Louis Vuitton* handbag. So it's high time we learn to draw the line and say, "Enough is enough!"

Most women in our generation have sometimes been taken for granted, especially if we sailed into adulthood embracing the traditional feminine role of putting everyone else's needs ahead of our own. After decades of being everyone's go-to nurturer, we practically forget that our lives are *ours* to live!

Time to flip the script.

Picture a forest after a raging fire. Would anyone in their

right mind expect it to be its usual shade-giving, oxygen-providing self? The same goes for anyone who still expects you to be Superwoman while your cape's in ashes.

Put your foot down and stop running on fumes to cater to everyone else. Right now, you need to guard your energy like it's the last slice of pizza at a *Super Bowl* party. Just like nature transforms a burnt-out forest into a green paradise, your hidden talents are ready to bloom when the time is right. Use this season to heal and rediscover yourself, and before you know it, your fresh growth will leave everyone—including you—in awe!

Now, in order to let that happen, you need to ace your MBA—Mastering Boundaries and Assertiveness, that is. A better life means knowing how to set boundaries like a boss. This doesn't mean becoming aggressive, pushy, or selfish. It means it's time to stop putting invisible duct tape over your mouth when you ought to speak up, or saying "Yes" to avoid confrontation or guilt. At first, assertiveness may take a bit of courage, but it's like a muscle that grows stronger and more agile with use. The key to setting boundaries is this: We can't communicate our boundaries to others until we've clearly communicated them to ourselves.

So, if any relationship in your life makes you feel like someone is constantly raiding your fridge without asking, it's time for some self-reflection. Get clear on what you will and won't tolerate and why. Then, take a cool, calm breath and make it known—no need for excuses or apologies.

Now, I know it can be challenging for many women of our generation to do this. A lot of us grew up without strong female role models. Plus, we've been expected to balance on a tightrope of likability while dodging bullets of intimidation and staying as warm and fuzzy as an Angora sweater. If the thought of enforcing your boundaries ever makes you freeze like a deer in headlights, remember, you're not *Bambi* anymore.

People may be surprised by the "new" assertive you. So what? They'll adjust as long as you aren't harsh or overbearing.

Approval addiction? Please! That's so last season. Disappointing people isn't a sin; it's a survival skill. Stand firm, and don't let people walk all over you like the red carpet at the Oscars. When it comes to commanding respect, the only obstacle that genuinely exists is you. So get used to standing up for yourself and master the art of "No."

Exercise 4: Boundaries & Assertiveness

Do you often find yourself saying "Yes" when you want to scream "No" louder than a toddler in a toy store? Don't worry, you're not alone. Let's dive into the fabulous world of setting boundaries with a smile. Self-awareness is the first step in learning how to assert yourself with the confidence of a diva demanding her dressing room be stocked with only green *M&Ms.*

- Are there specific situations where you find it hard to say "No"? Or particular people you find it hard to say "No" to? If so, list them.
- Do you hesitate to express your needs clearly and directly?
- Do you ever find yourself apologetic when requesting things you have every right to ask for?
- Do you find yourself pretending to agree with people you disagree with?
- What "white lies" do you tell other people?
- Why do you feel those "white lies" are necessary?
- What are some ways you can encourage more honesty in your relationships?
- What can you do to establish boundaries in your best interest, starting here and now?
- What is the worst thing that could happen if you set a boundary that disappointed someone?
- Can you recall a recent situation where you felt your boundaries were crossed?
- What can you do in a similar situation next time?

Remember, Ladies, setting boundaries isn't about being mean—it's about being smart. You deserve relationships that sparkle with honesty and respect.

4

Ignore Your Inner Imp

"You have power over your mind, not outside events.
Realize this, and you will find strength."
—MARCUS AURELIUS

Remember a time when someone said something to you that hurt more than stepping barefoot on a *Lego*? That jab probably made you see them as the Grinch who stole your self-esteem. But let's face it, Ladies, when it comes to cutting remarks, we're often our own harshest critics.

Our inner voices are more opinionated than a *Vogue* editor at a fashion show and more relentless than a New York City cabbie laying on the horn during rush hour. Science hasn't completely cracked the code on why we all have a little devil on our shoulder whispering sweet nothings of doubt and despair—sort of like having our own personal heckler on permanent retainer.

For the sake of this chapter, let's call that heckler the "Inner Imp." In addition to being relentless, she's as unreliable as a knockoff designer bag. And, if you haven't guessed, she's the architect of imposter syndrome. After all, the first word in imposter is *imp*.

As I mentioned in chapter 1, our brains tend to get stuck on repeat when they're playing our personal hit parade of self-doubts and insecurities. Enter our Inner Imp, who feeds off our anxieties like a kid at a candy buffet. She's got a whole repertoire of voices, from mimicking your mom to channeling that bully from middle school to sounding like your ex, etcetera.

Here's an example of how your Inner Imp works:

It's 7 a.m. You're all set to slay a presentation you've been perfecting for weeks. You got up early, ate a good breakfast, reviewed your notes, and put on a killer outfit. Your hair looks incredible, your makeup is flawless, and you're wearing just a hint of your favorite fragrance. As you grab your briefcase and glance in the mirror, your Inner Imp snarks, "You'll forget what you're supposed to say." Suddenly, you're jittery.

The Inner Imp is always ready to pounce. She acts like she's got a crystal ball and talks like she knows everything. But guess what? She's a total phony and about as original as a photocopier.

Here are some of her classic hits:

"It's too late for you to _________."
"Who's going to hire you?"
"You don't have talent."
"You'd better not try that. You'll make a fool of yourself."
"Why bother?"
"Women your age are invisible."
"You can't compete with_________."
"You look old."

"You look fat."

"You're not sexy anymore."

"You should have __________."

"You could never _______."

"You can't do anything right."

"You're awkward."

"You'll never find love again."

. . . Yawn . . .

Now, Ladies, I called this chapter "*Ignore* Your Inner Imp," not "*Escape* Your Inner Imp," for a reason. Escaping implies running away. Those who are forced to run are powerless. Instead of running, it's time to stand your ground and show that Inner Imp who's boss!

Next time she starts yapping away like a Chihuahua who just spotted the mailman, let out a sarcastic chuckle and say, "Thanks for sharing. Now zip it!"

Once you're on to her game, you have all the power in the world to shut her up.

Exercise 5: Ignore Your Inner Imp

- When does your Inner Imp get most aggressive?
- Whose voices does she speak in?
- Are there things you never told anyone?
- Does your Inner Imp ever use those secrets against you?
- Why are you keeping those secrets?
- What can you do to stop your Inner Imp from exploiting your secrets?
- Did anything you heard growing up empower your Inner Imp?
- What strengths did you acquire from your imperfect environment growing up?
- How can you use those strengths during this transitional time in your life?
- Knowing what you know now, how do you plan to treat your Inner Imp from now on?

5

Ask for Help

Ah, the world we live in with our fancy phones! It's like everyone always has a personal assistant, lifeline, and circus in their pocket. Thanks to this technology, we're inclined to ask *Google* for help before we ask each other.

Don't get me wrong—I love technology and independence. But there are times when taking on the world alone is about as bright as trying to mow your lawn with a pair of scissors.

For years, I took fierce independence to the extreme. Looking back, I now can see that approach to life made about as much sense as wandering around the house at midnight with all the lights off. It made me invisible, and I was guaranteed to trip sooner or later.

So, let's get real and acknowledge that all well-adjusted, successful people benefit from the support and cooperation of others. Often, it's a bit like a magic trick—they make what they're doing look easy, but there's more than meets the eye.

When it comes to that style of magic, women are often the invisible heroes behind the scenes. In fact, many of us get so used to being in the supporting role that it seldom occurs to us to lean on others when it's our turn.

But if you're serious about creating a fabulous future, asking for help is a life skill you need in your toolbox. In fact, the bigger your dream, the more cooperation you'll need to enlist. And hey, even Beyoncé has backup dancers!

Remember that bit from the *New Testament* book of *Matthew*? "Ask, and it will be given to you. . ." Believe it. And let's not forget that when you ask for help, you're actually giving others a chance to shine. People love to feel needed and appreciated.

Now, I didn't climb Mount Sinai to get this list, but here are my Ten Commandments for asking for help. Ladies, thou shalt observe them.

1. **Timing is everything.** Don't delay asking until you're in a bind and have to put someone in a "Do or Die" situation.
2. **Ask privately. Thank publicly.** Putting someone on the spot in front of others is tacky. Gratitude is always in style.
3. **Know *precisely* what you need before you ask.** Don't ask for so little that the help you receive doesn't do you much good. And, please, don't ask for the moon unless you're sure the person you're asking can easily hand you the moon—and you have a great plan for it.
4. **Choose carefully.** Don't always ask the same person; try to ask those who will likely find it easiest to help you.

5. **Never preface an ask with the words, "I hate to ask."** All that does is put the person you're asking in a position where they're obliged to both reassure you *and* help you.

6. **Be easy to help.** Make clear requests. Avoid monologues. Be poised to accept help. For example, if someone offers to pick you up at your home and give you a ride, be ready on time and know the exact address you're going to. If you need to borrow a little money, have Zelle, Cash App, Venmo, PayPal, or some other electronic transfer method at the ready, and have a plan to pay that money back.

7. **Expect a "Yes," but accept a "No" gracefully.** Guilt trips, bargaining, and pressure tactics aren't your fabulous style.

8. **Be Open-minded.** If someone you ask for help suggests you do something on your own as an alternative, hear them out. Being receptive to suggestions is a virtue.

9. **Clarify the terms of the favor up front in both directions:** no surprises, hidden strings, or regrets.

10. **Remember reciprocity.** If someone helps you, be willing to offer help, according to your ability, in return.

Remember: If you don't ask for something, you won't get it.

6

Ditch Difficult People

Fasten your seatbelts, Ladies, because we're about to traverse some rough terrain in our modern world where toxic people roam freely, spreading their nonsense far and wide. These folks come in all shapes and sizes, but they have one thing in common: crappy self-esteem. That's why they've cultivated the charming habit of sticking it to you when you're down. Many are verbal Ninjas in the art of passive aggression. You'll encounter them in your everyday life, lurking on social media, and sometimes in the media you consume. They could be your ex, former in-laws, so-called friends, neighbors, acquaintances, coworkers, employers, relatives, and, in some unfortunate cases, even your adult children. Yep, you heard me right.

They operate like wolves. Once they sense a hint of vulnerability, they swoop in and pounce like it's Black Friday at *Nordstrom*.

That's why they pose a particular threat to our mental and emotional health when we're recovering from a personal crisis. Toxic people thrive on exposing our flaws and resurrecting cringe-worthy memories like they're narrating a highlight reel of our life's bloopers.

If you find yourself being sucked into the morass of toxic interaction, and your attempts to turn it around are fruitless, say a graceful goodbye and go. You'll never move past your pain if the people you're around won't let you.

Some saboteurs masquerade friends until the moment we're no longer beneficial to them. At that point, their true colors come out. Another type will want to keep you forever in the second banana seat they reserved for you. They'll try to talk you out of your dreams faster than you can say, "I'm unworthy."

Ladies, don't you dare let anyone make you feel you don't deserve the life you want! And remember, anyone who can't tell the difference between friendship and fierce competition doesn't belong in your fabulous circle. You're embarking on a transformational journey, and if those frenemies can't handle playing nice, they've got to go!

On that same note, don't overshare your dreams. You don't have the time or energy to justify yourself to folks who can't see your vision and possibly couldn't even find their way out of a paper bag. Besides, you're too fabulous to let anyone goad you into a pointless argument.

Last but not least, if anyone tries to imply that the happiest and best parts of your life are behind you, don't stick around to argue. Cover your gorgeous ears, run a mile, keep calm, and carry on!

Remember: "No one can make you feel inferior without your consent."—Eleanor Roosevelt

Exercise 6: The Company You Keep

Legendary motivational speaker and author Jim Rohn said we have to ask ourselves three questions:

Who am I around?
How are they affecting me?
Is that okay?

Put pen to paper, ponder those crucial points, and make changes if warranted. Granted, you can't cut certain people out of your life entirely, but you can certainly minimize your exposure.

Needless to say, this exercise is for your eyes only.

7

Get Real

Grab your bathing suits, Ladies. It's time to take a deep dive into the whirlpool of our own personalities. Because let me tell you, unless you know who you truly are, you won't have a shot at making meaningful changes. It would be like trying to assemble an *Ikea* bedroom set without the instructions—you'd end up with a wobbly mess and extra parts you couldn't identify. Meanwhile, self-awareness is your backstage pass to power, stability, and fresh opportunities you have yet to imagine!

"Fake it till you make it" is a famous mantra, but pretending to have more confidence than we do won't fool anyone for long. If you don't believe me, think of that poorly assembled flat-pack furniture with its loose screws and wobbly legs. Looking back on my life, I wish I had spent less time pretending I had it all figured out, and more time admitting I didn't so I could actually get my act together. It took a multi-faceted crisis to understand that. But life is funny that way. Our toughest challenges often become the ones we're most grateful for later.

When life shatters you to pieces, one silver lining is the chance to see your flaws laid bare—sort of like taking an unintentional selfie. So, seize this pivotal opportunity and muster the courage to take a hard look at who you really are.

Now, looking inward is tricky because we have to take stock of three personas: who we think we are, who we really are, and who we aspire to become. To add to the confusion, all three of those opinionated gals speak to us in our own voice!

Meanwhile, in today's world, we don't have to look too far for encouragement to play the victim card and blame everyone and everything but ourselves for all our problems. Even if a lot of that blame is justifiable, you'll never be able to soar if you're toting around the dead weight of grudges and blame. And don't get me started on all the industries making a fortune on wounded women. From high-interest credit cards for "retail therapy" to alcoholic beverages with cute, girly names, to overpriced self-pampering, to self-help gurus who sell workshops and retreats on the premise that every unpleasant experience we've ever had qualifies as trauma or that some elusive being called "the inner child" is fully responsible for every wrong decision we've ever made.

There are loads of opportunists laughing all the way to the bank. But here's the bottom line: We need to face our mistakes head-on and hold ourselves accountable if we want to avoid repeating them. So, let's put aside the smoke and mirrors. It's the only way we'll ever take the reins of our lives and steer them where we want to go. And let me tell you, that's a journey worth taking.

The following exercise is designed for honest self-reflection.

Remember: You can be honest with yourself and still be kind.

Exercise 7: Get Real

"The Fault, Dear Brutus, is not in our stars but in ourselves."
—WILLIAM SHAKESPEARE IN *JULIUS CAESAR*

To paraphrase author Dan Brown, the trouble with putting a halo over our own head is that it doesn't have to slip very far to become a noose. So, instead of nominating ourselves for sainthood, let's drop the act and admit we're only human.

Pretending we're perfect is like airbrushing a zebra's stripes and calling it Thoroughbred. We're not fooling anyone, and we'll never win a race. So, let's take some time to reflect on these questions:

- Can you identify recurrent patterns in your life that have led to problems or challenges?
- Did you make any choices that contributed to your current problems?
- Are there ways in which you have avoided taking responsibility for your actions or decisions?
- Are there things you're doing now that are contributing to your problems?
- What's the smallest, easiest step you can take to improve or even eliminate one of those detrimental things now?
- Have any of your actions or attitudes negatively impacted your relationships? (As the wise Southern woman once said, "No pancake is so flat that it has only one side.")
- If so, imagine yourself in the other person's shoes for a moment. How would you have felt?
- What steps can you take to do better going forward?

8

Free Yourself

"We will either find a way or make one."
—Hannibal (Ancient Greece)

adies, you can't dazzle by sticking to the same tired old script. Let's break free of some self-limiting habits and elevate our game to enjoy life more.

Free Yourself from Worry.

When worries nibble at your psyche like a school of invisible piranhas, your first line of defense lies in language. Instead of saying, "I'm worried about _________," say, "I'm going to concern myself with __________."

Worry sees the problem, not the solutions. It leaves you at the mercy of whatever life throws your way. The minute you concern yourself, you take control.

Now, I get it. Worrying can become a habit, especially for us moms who spent years as the family's personal lifeguard, nurse, administrator, and crisis manager. But worrying about things beyond our control is like trying to orchestrate the weather. It won't work, and it will drive us crazy.

The "Worry Wednesday" Solution

Grab some slips of paper and write down your worries, one per slip. Put all of those slips into an envelope. Wait to open that envelope until the following Wednesday. After a week or so, when you look at those worries again, some will have probably taken care of themselves. As for the ones that are still there? Well, at least you'll face them with a little distance and a clearer head.

Free Yourself from TMI Temptation . . . and the Regret that Follows.

Ladies, no matter how overwhelmed you feel, you mustn't fall into the selfish habit of letting your own dramas, negativity, and fears hog the spotlight. Not only is it a surefire way to wreck your charm, but you might also have someone in your circle who is more interested in spreading gossip than lending a helping hand. So, save your dreary "tell-alls" for a counselor or a very close, trusted friend who's been there, done that, and has offered to be your sounding board.

In the same vein, Ladies, sometimes it's best to cut off a friend's oversharing session early—you don't want her cringing every time she sees you because she got too carried away dishing out all the juicy details.

Free Yourself from Angst.

Just as you can't walk around with blood oozing out of an open wound, you can't let your angst ooze out of your personality at every turn. Acknowledge your difficult emotions, own them, and find a place for them instead of letting them run your life. You could sweat them out in a Salsa class, ink them into a journal, brush them onto a canvas, belt them out on stage, and/or talk them out with a therapist. There's a time and place for everything—even rage and despair—but our moods are ours, and ours alone to manage. So try not to let them manage you.

Free Yourself from Toxic Social Media.

I'm not saying you can't dabble in a few platforms if it tickles your fancy. But for the love of *Chanel*, don't let those digital connections overshadow fundamental, face-to-face interactions with people who truly matter. And should you find yourself doomscrolling, getting mired in pointless conversations, arguing with fools, or cyberstalking your ex, it's time to unplug.

Free Yourself from the Wrong Therapist.

Some people toss around the "Get Therapy" line like it's a one-size-fits-all solution. But therapists aren't all alike, and finding the right one is essential. Pick someone you like being around, whose qualifications you trust, and whose ethics and methods jive with you. If you spill your guts to a therapist and feel that they're just not getting it or that their approach is straight out of a medieval torture chamber, look for someone else. Therapy can be pricey, but if your wallet feels a little light, don't fret—you have options:

Hotlines and Support Groups: These are often free and can provide immediate support and a sense of community.

Public Health Services: Many communities offer counseling services through public health clinics or community centers. Check out what's available in your area—you might be surprised by the resources you find.

Your House of Worship: If your spiritual home aligns with your beliefs and values, they may offer counseling services or support groups that could be just what you need.

And here's a little nugget of wisdom: No therapist expects your thoughts and emotions to be as tidy as a style blogger's walk-in closet. So don't treat your sessions like a Broadway audition or a final exam. Lay it all out there, keep it honest, and embrace the beautiful chaos with an open mind. It's in the messiness that the real magic happens.

Free Yourself from an Obsession with Closure.

Closure is such a buzzword these days, Ladies, but let's be honest. The bozos who hurt you? They're pros at deflecting. They have zero clue—or interest—in how they messed up your life. Seeking closure from them is like asking a snake for a hug.

Free Yourself from a Measly Income.

Money isn't everything, but it can be the best Band-Aid in a crisis. Unless you're rolling in dough, start thinking about fattening your piggy bank. Being short on dough forces you to make tough choices, constantly rethink your priorities, and stress over every dollar like it's the last lifeboat on the *Titanic*.

Thanks to my youngest daughter's suggestion, here's a one-two punch I used—one of the few things I nailed right off the bat. It was a total game-changer:

1. Get a notebook or a stack of index cards and start writing down at least one money-making idea every day. These can be businesses, services, inventions, products, jobs, gigs—the sky's the

limit. Never miss a day. Get creative. After all, you can't expect a Masterpiece if all you do is color inside the lines!

2. Go online daily and look for jobs, gigs, and side hustles, whether you think you need to earn more or not. A fun, part-time, or temporary job is a great way to earn, learn, and meet new people. Even if you're flush with cash, it's still better than lounging on your couch watching bad TV.

During the years when I was getting back on my feet, starting my business, *Savvy Civility*, and later, writing this book, I held down an array of gigs that included Brand Ambassador, Saleswoman, Actress, Freelance Writer, Air Conditioner Recall Repair Tech (Remove a part and replace it—my supervisor trained me), Focus Group Participant, Academic Competition Moderator, and Used Textbook Broker. Most of these gigs were short-term or intermittent, but having my hustle on kept me feeling young, vital, active . . . and making friends. I also bet my $1,200 COVID relief check on the stock market on a hunch that a new Telemedicine company would go big, and I made a tidy profit.

Ladies, there's nothing like having multiple income streams to make you feel safe and secure, so don't let ego or under-confidence undermine you.

If you're new to freelancing, hone your skills, set your rate, and present yourself as somebody who already earns that much. If you haven't worked in a while, apply for anything and everything while you up-skill. Before you know it, better money will come.

Free Yourself from Depressing Holidays.

After things go kablooey, holidays can feel more depressing than a rainy day at an abandoned amusement park, so plan ahead and do what suits you. If I can't be with my daughters on Christmas, I prefer a quiet day alone, dinner out with other "misfits," or volunteering over a traditional celebration at someone else's home. I've found that partaking in someone else's traditions and hearing them reminisce with their loved ones only reminds me of the birth family, marital family, and homes I lost. Now, that doesn't mean I'm sitting around moping—that's not allowed. Instead of letting sentimental days sneak up on me, I make a game plan and follow through with it, even if it takes some oomph. If you're facing major holidays alone, I suggest you do the same.

Here's the cherry on top of this self-liberation sundae:
Freeing yourself from all these burdens isn't about becoming a new you. It's about unleashing the *real* you—the fabulous, unstoppable force that's been long-buried under a pile of obligations and anxieties. Think of it as a decluttering spree for your soul, tossing out the junk and making room for the good stuff. No matter what may have happened in the past, this is a glorious new chapter.

Now that you're ready, it's time to step into your power and own every inch of it, so keep reading!

II

Step Into Your Power

"It's never too late to be the person you might have been."
—GEORGE ELIOT

This section is your rallying cry to think big, seize the day like it owes you money, and dream like nothing can stop you! And that's a big deal since, by and large, we women were socialized to give away our power like it's a party favor.

Thanks to that conditioning, whenever someone treats us like yesterday's leftovers, we tend to think we need to try harder, love more, give more, pray more, and wait for more. But we deserve better! So, let's reclaim our power and roll into every new situation like a marching band at a championship game.

Remember: Regretting the past is a waste of time. Real power lies in the here and now.

9
Fly Solo

"I won't need you to rescue me. I can take care of myself, thank you."
—Scarlett O'Hara in Margaret
Mitchell's *Gone with the Wind*

At first, flying solo in our Noah's Ark, two-by-two, society may feel unsteady. But once you embrace that you weren't born to be anyone's sidekick, you'll relish the freedom to do what you want when you want. You're now the undisputed star of your own show.

Still, I won't sugarcoat it. Being on your own is challenging until you get the hang of it. We're not talking about one big adjustment—we're talking about hundreds of little adjustments every day. But every slight adjustment you make is a victory that empowers you a little more.

The key ingredient to empowerment is self-perception, so let's chat about it for a moment. After all, self-belief is the secret to rocking your newly-minted life.

Now, no matter how you see yourself today, don't slap on a label—even if it's a good one. Here's why: Have you ever met someone who goes around calling themselves a "badass," "sexy," or "intellectual?" In time, they become a walking caricature of that label. That's because they grow to fit the mold and not one iota farther. Can you spell "Not fab?" Labels are for peanut butter jars, not great Ladies.

Likewise, we mustn't accept the labels people try to put on us. I'm not giving you this advice from a high horse. Thanks to my husband's dramatic exit, his flashy social media escapades with his "Miss Right Now" (who, by the way, could have been our daughters' classmate), his entourage of freeloading fast friends, our close-knit community, and his family's "blood is thicker than water" loyalty, I found myself tagged with a few unflattering labels during that first year when I was scrambling to keep my life on keel. When a long-married couple splits up over the husband's adultery, a surprising number of people indulge in schadenfreude towards his estranged wife.

Feeling outnumbered and vulnerable, with no family support (my parents and three of my four siblings had passed away years before), I found myself in a tough, confusing spot and had begun to self-isolate.

Then, one afternoon, a deep dig during a phone conversation pushed me to the edge. I rose up like a lioness, tore off the labels, and told that person—and not long after, everyone else involved in those reindeer games—to kiss my sass. Thanks to that newfound confidence, I stormed on with all the grace of a tornado in *Lululemon* leggings, redirecting my energy toward a comeback. And guess what? It didn't take long after that for my life to do a 180.

Ladies, take it from me, you owe it to yourselves to tear off the unflattering labels and flaunt your uniqueness like it's the latest trend everyone's dying to copy.

On that note, ready or not, you need to get out, mix and mingle.

Now's the time to reconnect with old friends and make new ones. Cultivating a solid support system is essential. Host dinner parties, go out for coffee, attend meetups, join clubs that interest you, and say "Yes" to invitations. At this point in our lives, friends are the family we choose, and believe me, it beats listening to Uncle Morty's political rants on Thanksgiving.

Beyond friends, you need to learn to enjoy your own company. For one thing, if you want to make a splash in the world or pick up some exciting new skills, you'll need to carve out some serious solo time for studying, practicing, working, and creating. All successful people have to pull a disappearing act from time to time. Becoming more than mediocre at anything is all about priorities.

However, there's a fine line between savoring your solitude and turning into a hermit crab, hiding away in your shell like it's a five-star resort. Alone time can be like a refreshing spa day for your soul, but complete reclusiveness is like living on nothing but celery and carrot sticks. It might seem healthy at first, but eventually, you'll start longing for some real flavor in your life.

So when you wake up alone on a weekend morning with nothing to do, put on something trendy and take yourself out for a spin, as if your life were a brand new *Audi* convertible on a sunny day. Hit up that cute little café where they sprinkle chocolate shavings on your latte like fairy dust. And don't you dare hide behind your phone like a security blanket—engage with the world around you, even if it's just swapping pleasantries with the barista.

Even if you're reluctant to attend an event alone, step into your big girl pumps and march your way through the door. You can leave early if you want, but the least you can do is grace the stage with a cameo appearance. At first you might feel like a fish out of water, but soon you'll be mingling, and in the swim as if the whole place were your private lagoon.

Once you get good at being on your own, both in social situations and in solitude, you'll enjoy a deep sense of emotional security that will carry you through all kinds of experiences.

So, grab life by the sequins and show the world what you're made of!

You heard me, Ladies. Time to put on something smashing and step boldly into the unknown!

10

Doohickeys, Gizmos, and Whatchamacallits

"We can do it!"
—ROSIE THE RIVETER

When you first start flying solo, Ladies, you'll soon realize your husband or partner was tackling chores you barely even knew existed. Time to roll up those sleeves—yes, even the designer ones—and learn to handle all those hidden tasks yourself.

Picture this: you wake up one morning ready to conquer the day like a boss, only to find out your toilet's overflowing, your car's thirstier than a Kardashian for attention, and Mother Nature decided to dump a blizzard on your doorstep. Being unprepared is like carrying around a laundry list of disasters waiting to happen.

Now, if your ex is living and you're on good terms, it's time to swallow that pride and ask for the lowdown on all those tasks they made look as easy as pie. If not, well, thank heaven for *YouTube!* It's a treasure trove of "how-to" videos just waiting to turn you into a DIY Diva. Believe it or not, you'll get emotional satisfaction from mastering new life skills. I'll never forget the day I walked into *Home Depot*, bought a monkey wrench, and replaced the gooseneck pipe under my bathroom sink. I felt like the coolest, most unstoppable chick on the block!

Here are a few basics. I suggest you learn how to do them *before* you're in a bind:

Home Maintenance Magic:

- Swap out furnace and air unit filters: Give your home a breath of fresh air!
- Reboot breakers and fuses: Hit the reset button and start anew.
- Cut power with electrical breakers: Say "lights out" to any electrical mishaps.
- Shut down the water main: Stop flooding at its source before it turns into Noah's Ark Part Two.
- Seal off water to toilets and sinks: Prevent leaks faster than a gossip columnist can spill a scandal.

Safety Chic:

- Keep a suitable fire extinguisher handy, and know how to use it like a pro.
- Test smoke alarms, carbon monoxide detectors, and security systems. Safety's always in style, Ladies.
- Sniff out gas leaks like a bloodhound on a scent.

Kitchen and Bathroom Brilliance:

- Clear a jammed garbage disposal: It's like removing a stubborn avocado pit—messy but satisfying!
- Drain a clogged toilet or sink: Clean those home arteries and keep the flow going!

Car Care Commandments:

- Check and top off oil: Keep your car purring like a kitten.
- Check tire pressure and add the right amount of air to roll along smoothly.
- Top off anti-freeze, coolant, and wiper fluid: Give your car a splash of refreshment and keep those windows sparkling!
- Have your vehicle professionally serviced on schedule.
- Keep these emergency essentials in your trunk: basic first aid kit, pair of old sneakers, jumper cables, spare tire, jack and lug wrench, multipurpose tool, flashlight with extra batteries, reflective warning triangles or LED signal lights, reflective vest, blanket or thermal blanket, umbrella or rain poncho, cell phone charger, ice scraper, tow rope, and, yes, I'm serious—a roll of duct tape. If you're going on a longer trip or regularly commuting through a rural area, throw in bottled water and non-perishable energy bars.

Now, even if you've got roadside service on speed dial—and I hope you do—there's no harm in knowing how to jump-start a car and change a flat tire. After all, self-reliance is always in style!

Rethinking Traditional Skills

While we're on the subject of chores, here's a point worth pondering. Many of us may have used our homemaking skills to assert our femininity. But let me tell you, Ladies, clinging to that outdated mindset is about as fashionable as shoulder pads, leg warmers, and frizzy perms.

At this stage in the game, there's no need to try to be the best at anything that doesn't light up your soul. Take it from me: After years of going all out like a Martha Stewart wannabe, I had an epiphany: Why complicate life when I could simplify it? I radically scaled down my cooking, left baking to the bakeries, and sold my sewing machine—So far, I love it!

Maybe you'd rather take a power walk than fold laundry, have your groceries magically appear at your doorstep as if by a fairy godmother, or pay someone to deep clean your home once or twice a month. If it'll put a skip in your step and you can fit it into your budget, why not? Embrace your inner diva and delegate like a boss!

Should something happen . . .

Now that you're flying solo, it's time to revisit your provisions for the loved ones you'll leave behind. If you've got your ducks in a row with an up-to-date will, burial insurance, and a Living Will, then kudos to you; you're ahead of the game. But if not, it's time to get your act together, pronto!

Let me tell you a little something from personal experience—I grew up in a family of seven and ended up burying five of them—four within a five-year window. Not exactly a task for the fainthearted. So please, whatever you do, don't leave your loved ones dealing with the tough decisions or costly arrangements you could have made ahead of time. It's a haunting problem nobody deserves while they're still reeling from your death or end-of-life status.

Get your paperwork in order, and for heaven's sake, let someone close to you know exactly where your Will, Burial Insurance, and Living Will are—and don't you forget Organ Donation details. Taking charge of your destiny isn't all about you. It also means leaving your loved ones with a little less to worry about when you're gone.

Here are the documents I'm referring to:

1. Your Will (if you have any financial or material assets.)
2. Your Living Will (A written statement detailing your wishes regarding your medical treatment in circumstances where you're incapacitated and unable to communicate.)
3. Your Medical Power of Attorney/Advance Directives—A document that provides a simple way to name someone you trust to speak to your healthcare providers and make decisions for you when you can't make or communicate those decisions for yourself.
4. Arrangements for your remains. If you want a traditional burial, get burial insurance and buy a cemetery plot. If you want to be cremated, get the paperwork and instructions in order. If you want your body donated to science, formalize your intent by registering with the Science Care online donor registry, the United Tissue Bank, or a similar organization.

If you want complete, easy-to-follow advice on getting your affairs in order, I highly recommend the book *Because It Matters* by Cheyenne R. Mease.

Remember: Nothing beats knowing you're the captain, the crew, and the air traffic controller of your own journey.

Exercise 8: Fly Solo

- What are some things your partner used to do for you that you're now doing for yourself?
- What new skills have you gained?
- How does that new self-reliance feel?
- What personal qualities are emerging or strengthening during this new solo chapter of your life?
- What are some positive things about becoming more independent?
- What additional things will you have to do for yourself in the future?
- If you don't know how to do those things, how do you plan to learn?

11

Rediscover U

Can we talk about this whole concept of *"reinventing yourself?"* I'm not a fan. That term makes us sound like we're outdated software waiting for the latest upgrade. It's not just absurd—it's insulting! Granted, life can get messier than a teenager's bedroom, and years of obligations can bury our true selves deeper than the lost city of Atlantis, but that doesn't mean we need to start over from scratch.

So, think of "Rediscover U" as a university without walls, admission criteria, or tuition fees. You stand to benefit whether you're a rugged contrarian, a card-carrying conformist, or anywhere in between.

I happen to believe God crafted each of us with love and

genius and that every human being is a masterpiece. Our job? To embrace what we were given at birth and do all we can to make the most of it.

The phrase "Be yourself" is tossed around so much that it's practically background noise, and besides, it's meaningless unless you know who you are. But when you truly know yourself, you stand firm in your identity and attract and gravitate toward the people, places, things, and ideas that are best for you.

We all know that women's lives change more than men's. On top of that, as I've mentioned before, we become experts at rising to every duty demanded of us. In time, putting ourselves last becomes our default behavior. We serve ourselves the lopsided pancake, sit through the boring movie our husband and kids want to see, take the uncomfortable folding chair at the holiday table, and on and on. When we're suddenly single, all those years of playing "How Can I Sacrifice More?" takes a toll on our ability to live for ourselves . . . until we get our minds around our new freedom.

Those same responsibilities often require us to shove our talents and interests into a mental storage locker. Ladies, it's time to unlock that storage locker and sort through those bundles of beginnings and deferred dreams.

Fundamental to this process is taking a long look back and thinking about your life before romance and all that fanfare took over.

Can you remember who you were between about the ages of six and ten? Odds are that's when you were your most authentic self—fearless, not too worried about your looks, and ready to take on the boys in any competition. And it's not just me reminiscing about my childhood, my daughters, or what I observed when I was a Girl Scout leader—there's actual science behind this.

In their fascinating book, *The Confidence Code,* researchers Kay and Shipman found that up until age eight, girls have as much self-confidence as boys. However, their self-confidence drops by 30% between the ages of eight and fourteen. So unless you're a rare exception, your self-confidence probably took a nosedive in Middle School, too.

But I'll bet my bottom dollar that vibrant little girl is still sleeping within you. Maybe she painted, excelled at sports, loved science, or had a way with animals . . . .

Once you reawaken her, you'll tap into a fascinating cache of forgotten talents and half-opened gifts in your heart, mind, and soul. That's where the magic lies. Best of all, your wisdom, maturity, experience, and grown-up self-discipline will turbocharge your interests and abilities. I'm convinced our true purpose in life involves embracing our authentic selves. That's where we find the things we do easily, naturally, and better than most while barely breaking a sweat. So dig deep, reacquaint yourself with that uniquely gifted little girl you used to be, and give her the opportunity to rise and shine!

We all have our gifts.

Some women find hosting a dinner party more stressful than a root canal. They plan and agonize for days, cook up something mediocre, and need a week to recover. Other women can whip up a feast on a whim and feel extra energized the next day. Some women can play jazz tunes on the piano by ear, while others take lessons for months and can barely manage "Twinkle, Twinkle Little Star"—you get the picture. With fewer years ahead of us and more experience behind us, we owe it to ourselves to embrace and play to our strengths.

Moving into your gifts will make you happier and more fulfilled, and in time, it might also make you money. And don't worry if you don't have classical training. Inventors who never studied engineering, singers with quirky voices, and artists who won't rival Michelangelo have all found massive success. If they can boldly embrace their vision and harness their strengths, so can you!

Of course, no matter how much talent you've got, you'll only succeed if you persist. But Ladies, you have a moral obligation to be extraordinary because there'll never be another you. The world needs what you—*and only you*—have to offer!

Did you wake up this morning? If the answer is "Yes," that's a pretty good sign that God has more for you to do here on earth. So, tie up your hair and get cracking!

Of course, as you rediscover yourself, be prepared to change. Purpose-driven women tend to guard their time and energy. They find it easy to say "No" to things that don't align with their goals.

If this chapter left you uncertain about rediscovering yourself, don't worry. The following exercises are designed to help you with that process.

Exercise 9: Rediscover U

Take out your pen and paper and reflect on the time before you entered your teens.

- What year or years were your happiest?
- Your strongest?
- Your smartest?
- Your least self-conscious?
- Who was your favorite teacher?
- Who were your best friends?
- What were your favorite activities?
- What was your favorite subject in school?
- What books, songs, and shows did you like best?
- What famous person did you admire most?
- Where did you love to go?
- What kind of future did you imagine for yourself?
- What were your wildest dreams?
- Have you ever heard an inner voice saying, "This is what you should do!" If so, what did that voice tell you?
- When do you trust yourself the most?
- Is there/was there anything that people have always told you about yourself or even teased you about? Believe it or not, that trait might be your biggest talent in disguise.
- If you can access your old report cards, photos, and school projects, revisit them.
- What subject were your best grades in?

If you're like me, your grades could have been better across the board. Even so, I have no doubt there were one or two subjects you found easiest and most interesting. If your report cards show some subjects you did poorly in, it's possible you were daydreaming in those classes. If so, do you remember what you were thinking about that made it hard to pay attention?

Whether you were the class clown, the fastest in the 50-yard dash, a math whiz, the scout who sold the most cookies, or one of a thousand other things, you were born with natural gifts.

What common themes do you see when you look at your answers to these questions?

Maybe everything you excelled in and loved was creative, mathematical, involved teamwork, or carried a sense of adventure or nurturing. The possibilities are almost endless.

Is that common theme playing out to your satisfaction in your life today? If you're one of the few people who can answer that last question with a resounding "Yes," and you feel you're living up to your potential, congratulations! If not, your life will be more worthwhile and have a greater impact on the world if you start moving into alignment with your authentic self.

Once you commit your heart and mind, it'll probably be a short distance between taking the first step in rediscovering what you were born to do and being pleasantly surprised by your talent.

12

Commit to Your Dream

*"Everything is in the mind. That's where it all starts.
Knowing what you want is the first step toward getting it."*
—MAE WEST

Now that you're all dressed up and stepping into your power, it's time to go after that dream. Not in the manner of those unfocused dreamers who'd rather chase their tails like a pack of excited puppies in a pet store window than get serious. But like a strong, determined woman who sits down and commits to what she truly desires.

Finding the right dream for you is like searching for that perfect pair of jeans. You'll get better results if you're purposeful, persistent, and picky. You can't just wander around like you're lost in a mall, hoping to find your dream somewhere between the Food Court and *Forever 21*.

Think of your dream as a secret recipe handed down from the universe's top chef and meant just for you. It's a whisper from the divine, guiding you toward your purpose. Your imagination is that divine spark within you, ready to light your unique path.

If you're still skeptical about the power of dreams, take a moment. Look all around you. Everything, from the building you're in, to the clothes on your back to the furniture you're sitting on, to this very book, once merely danced in someone's imagination.

We all can realize things we envision if we embrace our talents, put in the elbow grease, and stay the course. As Thomas Edison famously quipped, "Genius is one percent inspiration, ninety-nine percent perspiration." So remember, Ladies, dreams are nothing without action. It's time to prioritize, commit, and make your dreams a reality.

So, step by step, let's get a crystal-clear vision of what you want most.

1. **Cut Through the Haze**: It's sort of like cleaning a closet—time to sift through all those notions, wishes, and whims. Toss out what no longer fits or suits you and organize the rest into something coherent.

2. **Embrace Your Inner Weirdo**: Drop the notion that your dream needs to be grandiose or universally admired. Maybe you dream of becoming the world's best cat whisperer, writing rap songs in Esperanto, or opening a bath boutique that specializes in artichoke soaps. Whatever it is, *own it*. The more specific and peculiar your dream, the more it's truly yours.

3. **Play the "What If" Game** as many times as it takes. Ask yourself, "What do I want?" Write it all down. Remember, this list is for your eyes only. Revisit that list again and again. Picture yourself in each dream scenario. If imagining yourself there makes you feel like you've just had three espressos, you're on

the right track. If it feels like sitting through a three-hour lecture on the history of paperclips, let it go. Some people say our dreams indicate what God has prepared for us. Whether you believe this or not, taking your dream seriously is essential. Don't make the mistake of picking a pipe dream you'll never go after or of dreaming too small. Choose an exciting dream that gives you room to grow.

4. **Get Specific**: Once you've narrowed it down, put everything on paper, either in writing or on a vision board where you can see it. If, for example, you dream of living in New York City, picture the neighborhood, building, and apartment and how you'll decorate it down to the last throw pillow. Dreams are like a packet of seeds—if you want Zinnias, you have to plant Zinnia seeds instead of Petunias. They won't bloom overnight, but with the proper care, you'll see progress . . . which brings us to Step 5.

5. **Get Serious**: Pursuing a dream doesn't mean ignoring reality; it means working with it. If you aim to soar, forget the flighty fantasies and think about the logistics. Do you need Education? Training? Funding? Etc. Create a plan that includes small, manageable steps. Contrary to certain trending gurus, you can't just manifest your dreams into reality by thinking. When you catch yourself drifting off into La-La Land, treat those flights of fancy like the words of a whimsical child spinning tales about turning a cardboard box into a rocket to the moon. Smile to yourself and say, "How creative! Thanks for sharing," then row your boat back to reality, roll up your sleeves, and get to work.

6. **Don't Tell Your Dream to Everyone**: Surround yourself with people who believe in you, and give dream crushers the distance you'd give someone who hasn't discovered deodorant.

If Oprah had listened to the haters, she'd be working as a cashier in a supermarket instead of ruling the media world.

7. **Stay Optimistic:** No matter how old you are, don't think for a nanosecond that you missed the boat or fell off the track. Laura Ingalls Wilder started writing the *Little House on the Prairie* series at 65. Julia Child hit our TV screens as *The French Chef* when she was 51. Grandma Moses first picked up a paintbrush at 78 and became a prosperous, world-renowned artist by her early 80s.

8. **Stay Focused:** Though we may have varied interests and talents, going after too many things simultaneously is like trying to knit a sweater with spaghetti—messy, confusing, and it won't work. So focus your energy, Ladies. If you don't, you'll accomplish a whole lot of nothing.

9. **Celebrate Small Wins:** It's the only way to stay motivated and remind yourself you're making progress. Nothing can hold you back once you feel like a winner in your heart. You'll soon stretch yourself in ways you never thought possible, meet folks who'll change your life, and revel in that exhilarating sensation of momentum.

Last But Not Least . . . pursuing a dream is as much about the journey as the destination. Laugh at the mishaps, cherish the learning moments, and be proud of yourself for embarking on one of your life's most extraordinary adventures!

Remember this simple recipe: Faith, Focus, and Fortitude in equal parts.

13

From Dreamer to Doer

You must be present to win.

Don't worry if you still feel a little uncertain about direction. After all, if you want to find gold and diamonds without a treasure map, you'll have to do some prospecting. But you can only do that if you show up. As long as you don't invest more time or money than you can afford to lose, there's no harm in exploring a direction or two that might not pan out. Testing a few wild ideas and having a few failed experiments is a commendable part of the journey. That said, avoid getting stuck in the loop of experimenting for years. Success requires consistency, even on days when staying focused is more challenging than finding a cab in the rain.

Now, let's admit it, we've all been there. We tell ourselves we'll chase our dreams once we've got more time, practice, confidence, money, you name it. But let me hit you with some truth bombs: you'll never feel completely ready, and there'll never be a flawless moment.

Assuming you're not aiming to become a teen pop star, an Olympic gymnast, or a Navy SEAL, it's safe to say you have a shot at just about anything you set your mind to—but only if you set your mind.

Doers understand there will always be obstacles and that even the most successful people stumble. They dive in, knowing they'll figure it out along the way. Dreamers, on the other hand, wait for the elusive perfect moment that never arrives.

Imagine if Ella Fitzgerald, Mama Cass Elliot, Queen Latifah, or Adele had decided they couldn't sing in public until they rocked a slim figure. They'd have been belting it out in the shower forever! Instead, they cranked up their plus-size talent and blasted off into stardom. As the saying goes, "You'll either find a way or find an excuse." So, if you're 75% ready to go after something, it's time to dive in! If not, figure out what you need to do and do it.

By now, I've lost count of the people who learned I was writing a book and told me they're going to write one, too, as soon as they had time. *News Flash:* I didn't have time either. That's why this book took five years. Ladies, little steps will eventually get you where you want to go. Inaction won't get you anywhere. It's easy to blame inaction on a lack of time, but let's face it, we all have the same 24 hours in a day—unless you're living on another planet . . . and if that's the case, call me! We need to chat!

The point is, if you're passionate about something, you make time for it. Whether it means sacrificing something else or squeezing in a few minutes here and there, follow what you love, and love will find a way—even if it has to break down walls with a sledgehammer. If money's an obstacle, get creative and find a hustle, a benefactor, a barter, or a workaround. And if fear's holding you back, do it scared! Remember the words of Barbara Sher, "Fear is just excitement in a bad makeup job."

Consider this. Right now, I have no idea how many people will read this book. But if I want to be certain, all I have to do is quit writing today. Then, I'll have zero readers.

Quitting is for women who want to live and die blending in with the wallpaper. That's not what we're put on this earth to do. So, Ladies, let's stop waiting for perfection and start making progress. Dive in, make waves, and soon enough, you'll start to show up big—wherever you are.

Getting Your Dream into Focus

One perk I enjoyed when doing a lot of work as a freelance writer was interviewing successful people. The biggest through-line I've seen in their stories isn't talent or privilege—it's clarity of vision. That clarity appears to work like a GPS, directing them toward their dreams with a mix of inspiration and tenacity. A clear dream will attract you, like the Christmas windows at *Bergdorf's*. Even the tiniest step closer is as smile-inducing as finding a wad of cash in your old jeans or learning your favorite shade of lipstick hasn't been discontinued after all. And that energizing clarity can even turn a long-deferred dream into an achievable goal.

For me, that forgotten dream was acting. Twenty-some years after quitting acting to be a wife and mother, I saw a community theater audition notice for the drama *I Never Saw Another Butterfly*, which tells the true story of children in the Terezin Concentration Camp during World War II. I had read the play as a teenager and had always dreamed of being in it but never had the opportunity. By the time I was fifty-plus, just mustering up the courage to read for a community play felt like scaling a mountain, but I did it anyway. To my astonishment, I was cast as Irena Synkova, the teacher who surreptitiously taught the children to draw and paint in those unthinkable circumstances. Performing on the community stage reignited a spark I thought had long gone out. I once again started to think of myself as an actress and began working on my craft.

Six years and many shows and projects later, I found myself in a small role in the courtroom drama *Chasing Jack* at the Orbach Theater Center on 50th and Broadway in New York City, which ran for six months. Though I hadn't mentioned it to anyone, I had always dreamed of acting on a New York stage. It was exciting when that long-deferred dream came true, if even for just a few lines.

Ladies, if I can dust off decades-old acting chops, get back in the mix, and pull it off, you, too, can—and should—go after whatever has been hidden in your heart.

Keep your dream close to the vest.

As I mentioned before, do yourself a favor and zip those lips when it comes to your dreams. Sharing your dream with most people is like handing a priceless vase to a toddler. They won't understand it, and there's a good chance they'll shatter it into pieces.

And as to telling your friends your dreams to create account-ability? That can be a one-way ticket to Anxiety Town. It's like giving your GPS to a backseat driver—and telling them to make you second-guess every turn.

Last but not least—and we'll get into this in more depth later—our subconscious mind is as literal as a robot. It can't differentiate between a speculative statement and reality. So, when you blab about your dream and get some affirmation, your subconscious mind thinks you've already accomplished it. I don't know of a trickier motivation dampener than that.

Now, if you can find a seasoned mentor who's walked the path you're dreaming of, make an exception to the "keep mum" rule.

Otherwise, save your words, put in the work, and let your success do the talking.

We're Amazingly Adaptive!

Before we move on, I'll share a little tale from the high seas. Years ago, my then-husband signed us up for a sailing course. Let me clue you in on sailing: pun intended—it's not a breeze. It has its own language, and handling a sailboat takes more mental and physical strength and agility than I had expected. So, guess who was the slowpoke in that class? Yours truly. Even though I didn't turn into a seasoned sailor, I had a great time.

So, what makes sailing so captivating? Picture this: a dozen sailboats in a marina, gliding gracefully in all directions while using the same wind. No matter which way the wind blows, a skilled sailor can steer the boat anywhere just by adjusting the sails. Sure, using sailing as a metaphor for adaptability isn't groundbreaking—authors, psychologists, and motivational speakers have all navigated these waters. But I love it because I've experienced it firsthand, and it's such a vivid and inspiring image.

To be sure, the winds of change are blowing, but that doesn't mean we have to be pushed off course or stay anchored in one spot. We can harness that power to navigate our own path. So, hoist those sails, Ladies, and embark on your journey! Your dreams are calling from just beyond the horizon. Anchors away, with the wind in your hair and a spirit of adventure in your heart!

Remember: There's always more than one way to reach your dreams, so if you feel you're at an impasse, ask yourself, "What are *all* the ways I can make this happen?"

14
Sync with Your Set

"You are only going to be as good as the people you surround yourself with,
so be brave enough to let go of those who keep weighing you down."
—Ziad K. Abdelnour

We already discussed who to avoid. But surrounding yourself with the right people is the secret to living your best life. As Plato said, relationships are our soil. None of us deserve to be planted in dirt that leaves us wilting.

Though you're the star in the grand drama of your life, let's remember the importance of the supporting cast. Have you ever heard you're the average of the five folks you spend the most time with? Believe it. Scientists tell us we're wired to mirror those around us. It's like our prehistoric ancestors copying the tribe's top dog to survive. Even though we're living in the 21st Century, we still do it, even if we're unaware of what we're doing.

So, want to boost your IQ? Buddy up with brainiacs. Craving

more fun? Mix with mirth-makers. Want to be more active? Fraternize with fitness fanatics. Love a full calendar? Wing it with social butterflies. Looking for excitement? Seek out adventure enthusiasts. Chasing career success? Mingle with movers and shakers. Want to strut like a style icon? Team up with the trendsetters. You get the gist.

Whether it's mastering a foreign language or waltzing your way into ballroom dancing, aim up. Find a challenging group. You'll sweat a bit more, but it'll be worth it! And who says you can't juggle more than one social circle? Think of your social life as a water barrel; you need to let out some old stale water and let some fresh water circulate in to keep the whole barrel fresh. If you don't, eventually, everything will get murky and unpleasant. So don't be afraid to pull the plug on those toxic connections and shake it up! Add a splash of new faces, mix in a bit of excitement, and watch your sphere of friends become as refreshing as a crystal-clear spring in an oasis.

Once you're chasing your dream, get to know some folks who've already found success in the same arena. You'll always benefit from a good mentor, even if you live to become a fabulous centenarian. And remember, mentors and inspiring friends aren't just flesh and blood. They live in books, on *YouTube* videos, on TV, on the radio, and everywhere in between. If a historical figure captures your imagination, dive into their autobiography. Reading the words of an inspiring person is like having a tête-à-tête with them. Pick different mentors for different qualities—mixing things up keeps life exciting!

As you gather your circle of mentors, remember that throughout our lives, we'll bump into thousands of people each having a different role in our lives. Sometimes, we shine like the sun; other times, we're like the moon, reflecting the glow of those around us. Both roles have their time and place, but watch out for those dim bulbs who do nothing but cast shadows and try to eclipse you. You don't need shade when you're aiming for the stars. Choose stellar friends and associates and shine on!

Exercise 10: Sync with Your Set

Write down the names of. . .

- A friend or two who makes you feel great about yourself.
- A friend or two who makes you feel optimistic.
- A friend or two who makes you laugh.
- A friend or two who inspires you to improve yourself in some way.
- A friend or two who could use a little help or attention from you.

This week, pick up your phone and get in touch with each of those friends. If you're in the same town, make plans to get together. If you're far apart, schedule an online chat.

15

Be True to Your Code

"Before I can live with other folks, I've got to live with myself."
—Atticus Finch in Harper Lee's
novel *To Kill a Mockingbird*

As we plunge deeper into the wild waters of self-discovery, let's discuss your principles. They warrant center stage. So, let's give a round of applause to this diva of your identity—Ms. Moral Code.

Major turning points are a good time for us to reexamine our principles. People who never do this get dragged through life like a limp marionette at a puppet show, and trust me, that's no way to live. As Socrates famously said, "The unexamined life is not worth living."

So grab that metaphorical thinking cap—preferably something chic—while opening your heart wide. Suppose we start with the *Golden Rule?* Essentially, it's "Treat others the way you want to be treated." It's a simple and universal ethical principle that transcends religious and cultural boundaries.

The dilemma here can be that the Golden Rule can sometimes lead to too much self-sacrifice if you always prioritize others' needs over your own. Fairness includes being fair to yourself, so it's important to balance empathy with healthy boundaries.

With all that in mind, think about your recent interactions with family, friends, coworkers, neighbors, and even strangers. Are you kind, respectful, fair, and honest with yourself and others? Would you be satisfied if someone treated you the way you treated them in a similar situation?

Next, think about the moral principles you've inherited. Do any feel outdated or misaligned with your current values and beliefs? If so, are they rooted in family traditions, cultural norms, or religious teachings? Understanding their origins can help you decide what to keep, modify, or discard. If you want to build a dazzling new life, it needs to stand on your true blue, rock-solid moral foundation. No hand-me-down principles here!

Spirituality

I'm not here to tell you what to believe. There are over 4,000 religions in this big, wild world—and a sea of agnostics and atheists to boot. I've always had faith, but I've met plenty of good people who swear they don't have a drop. I have also met some folks who had faith but didn't know it. Their faith was in the form of fear, which amounts to faith that things will go wrong.

Faith is freedom.

No matter where you stand on the big guy upstairs, you can't live a meaningful life if every day feels like a roller coaster ride with no safety bar and you have no opinion about why you're here or where you're headed.

If scriptures aren't your thing, crack open some philosophy

books or attend lectures and discussion groups that get your brain buzzing. Are you struggling because you feel the joke's on you? Read the Absurdists like Camus, ponder with the Nihilists like Nietzsche, or get existential with Sartre. Want to be well-rounded? Mix it all up and then some!

Dive into whatever ideas spark your mind, and decide whether or not you think they're true and whether or not they matter.

Not into praying? Throw some affirmations and grateful vibes into the universe.

Don't want to meditate? Take a walk in the great outdoors and let nature do its thing.

If you're still searching, chat with folks from different faiths and visit various houses of worship. Your spirit needs care and keeping no matter what you believe.

Discover your sacred words—whether from scripture, literature, history, biography, poetry, or the memory of a loved one. Tuck them into your mind and heart verbatim. They're your secret weapon, ready to spring forth whenever you need them most.

Stay curious and in awe of whatever cosmic power is steering our mind-boggling universe.

Respect others' rights to their beliefs instead of becoming so narrow-minded, you can't see the forest for the trees in humankind's quest for meaning. Whatever you believe, don't let it turn you into an uptight, overbearing, self-righteous bore.

After all, society has gone through a complete makeover in our lifetime—sort of like going from black-and-white TV to virtual holograms in every color of the rainbow. Whether you're rocking traditional values, non-traditional vibes, or a mix of both, adopting a live-and-let-live approach will save you more drama than a soap opera marathon. On that note, if you get invited to partake in something that doesn't fit into your spiritual and moral puzzle,

"No thanks" is all you need to say. If they continue to push, just say, "It's not my style," and leave it at that. It's not our job to reform anyone; just focus on doing what's best for you.

And while we're talking about belief systems, look at the big three: Jesus, Buddha, and Gandhi. They all ditched material possessions to find enlightenment. That aspect of their lives came to my mind after I lost many of my earthly possessions in a twist of fate. Using their stories as a mental anchor made me feel chosen instead of cursed.

A few years later, I sold everything I had left, except what fit into a few suitcases, and set off on a nomadic journey for freedom, adventure, and spiritual growth. It was a radical move, and it's not for everyone, but it was suitable for me. Ever since I was cast out of "*Stepford*" and all its upscale suburban trappings, adaptability has been my ticket to growth. But again, what works for one person might not work for another. Each of us must find and follow our unique path.

Speaking of paths, even if you live in a resplendent home full of priceless heirlooms, I suggest you pack a simple travel bag and escape those posh surroundings every now and then. Even if your grand adventure is just an unplugged weekend in a fishing cabin down the road, you'll come back with clarity, serenity, and a fresh perspective.

So there you have it, Ladies! Stand by your principles, live authentically, and don't be afraid to sprinkle in a little sass along the way. After all, the world needs more fabulous women of substance who have done enough inner work to truly dance to the beat of their own drum—preferably in fun fashions!

But wait. I'm not letting you off with paying lip service to something so important. The following pages contain a three-part exercise about defining your values. It's a little work, but the self-knowledge you'll come away with is worth it.

Exercise 11: Define Your Values

A Three-Part Reflection

Part One: Contains a list that amounts to a smorgasbord of things people value and prioritize. At first glance, you might say, "Everything on that list is important to me!" I understand, but no two people are alike; everyone cares more about certain things than others.

Take a hard look at this list because some of your priorities might have been imposed on you without you even realizing it. Maybe you're trying to impress certain people or live up to some glossy, picture-perfect ideal. Been there. Done that!

When I was married, I thought my house, my car, and how I dressed and entertained were part of my identity. After my financial and material world turned upside down, I had to rethink my values. Surprise, surprise! Many of the things I thought were important didn't matter to me at all. They were just superficial trappings of someone else's idea of an attractive wife, a devoted mother, a successful daughter, a thoughtful daughter-in-law, a respectable community member, and so on.

When you look over the list, trust your gut, take your time, and don't be self-conscious about whatever floats your boat. Choose the twenty things that matter most to you, knowing nobody else will see your choices. Once again, it doesn't mean the other things don't matter. It just means they don't make the top twenty.

Defining and articulating your values is essential to creating the life you want.

Imagine you're a pioneer packing your life into a Conestoga wagon setting out to cross the prairie or an immigrant packing a trunk for the journey by steamship with limited space. You've only got room for twenty top picks. Make 'em count!

Between You and Yourself . . . What 20 things on this list do you value *most*?

1. Close Friendships
2. Networking
3. Mature Love
4. Romantic Love
5. Dating
6. Sex
7. Independence
8. Self-Respect
9. Freedom
10. Social Recognition
11. Professional Status
12. Affluence
13. Wisdom
14. Faith / Spirituality / Religion
15. Family Security
16. Material Security
17. Sense of Accomplishment
18. Creature Comforts
19. Tranquility
20. Excitement
21. Challenge and Ambition
22. Creative Expression
23. Intellectual Development
24. Fitness
25. Personal style and beauty
26. Attractive home
27. Achievements
28. Activity / Staying Busy
29. Adventure & Excitement
30. Amusement / Entertainment / Fun
31. Feeling of belonging
32. Open-Mindedness
33. Career Opportunities
34. Caution
35. Cleanliness
36. Altruism and Community Service
37. Conservation
38. Social Justice
39. Continuous Improvement
40. Education
41. Quality Time with Grown Children / Grandkids
42. Entrepreneurship
43. Focus on Future
44. Frugality
45. Generosity
46. Gratitude

47. Hedonism
48. Home
49. Hospitality
50. Inner Harmony
51. Inspiration
52. Integrity
53. Travel
54. Making a difference
55. Mindfulness
56. Openness to Change
57. Openness to Experience
58. Optimism
59. Order & Organization
60. Passion
61. Persistence
62. Personal Development
63. Personal Growth
64. Playfulness
65. Politeness
66. Popularity
67. Positivity
68. Recognition
69. Recreation
70. Refinement
71. Relaxation
72. Respect
73. Self-Control
74. Self-Direction
75. Self-Reliance
76. Sense of Humor
77. Other? __________

Part Two: Answer the following questions.

- What current activities are you engaged with that align with your top 20 values?
- Are you living in a way that honors your top 20 values?
- What can you do or participate in to align your life more closely with your top 20 values?
- What are you spending time on now that doesn't align with your top 20 values?
- What can you do to change that?

Part Three:
List five people you admire and what makes them admirable in your eyes.

Next, imagine you've kicked the bucket, and people are reminiscing about you. What traits do you hope they'll be raving about? Are there one or two areas where you ought to level up?

Remember: If you want to enjoy the confidence that comes with integrity, treat anything that clashes with your values like a bad fashion accessory.

16

Draft a New Blueprint

"Freedom is the will to be responsible for ourselves."
—FRIEDRICH NIETZSCHE

Ladies, if you're still with me, you're ready for the book's cornerstone premise: **You can't build a new life within the framework of the past.**

By midlife, most of us are set in our ways, and I'm sorry to say we may still be thinking, saying, and doing some things that are as outdated as a rotary phone.

But once the proverbial wrecking ball has whacked your world, you can't just slap on a Band-Aid and call it a day any more than a construction crew can rebuild a half-collapsed building with Elmer's Glue and popsicle sticks.

It's time to set aside the outdated blueprints and design a new life that sets your soul on fire! But hold your horses; that doesn't mean you should start tearing down walls willy-nilly. You have to gather your materials and sketch out a plan. The goal? A life that makes you want to high-five yourself every morning. Trust me, it's worth every ounce of effort.

Being the architect of your new life is like building your dream house. You might not need a moat or a turret—unless you're really into that—but you do need a solid foundation, fabulous decor, and a layout that makes you want to host a dinner party every night. Think of this process as your personal *HGTV* show, except the prize at the end is a life that's not just livable but utterly lovable.

And don't worry if you hit a snag here or there. Even the best home makeover episodes have their hiccups. Remember, Rome wasn't built in a day. So grab your metaphorical hammer, put on your most stylish hard hat, and let's get to work! After all, the only thing standing between you and a life that makes you do a happy dance is a bit of brainpower and elbow grease.

A Cautionary Tale From My Own Playbook

When my marriage bit the dust, and I lost my cozy nest, I made the rookie mistake of trying to recreate a single, empty-nester's version of my old life. I rented a good-sized house with a yard and the whole bit. I brought my half of the furniture and artwork I had bought with my husband when we were still in our happy thirties with a young family—and then I added to it by way of a shopping spree at the antique mall. I cooked full meals every day and decorated for the holidays the same way I had for years.

Spoiler alert: That year was a lonely, depressing, costly disaster. To this day, I avoid looking back on it.

I was trying to pour new wine into old wineskins, and let me tell you, it tasted stale! When my lease was up, I sold the furniture and rented a furnished room in a condo with a recent divorcee my age named Sylvia.

Not only were we both starved for fun, but we wanted to build our social circle, so we created a tradition called "Salon Saturday." Once a month, we each invited friends in for a casual lunch. The cost of admission? Every guest had to get up and perform or present something. They could tell a joke or a story, sing a song, show us something they had created, teach a mini-lesson, etc. Ukulele solos, quick sketches, Tango dancing, poetry recitations, and more entertained us. That year bore no resemblance to my married years, and it was, far and away, one of the best of my life.

But, of course, we both moved on. Sylvia remarried and moved to another town. I bought a dilapidated condo on the cheap and made it beautiful—and nothing like my marital home. The lock-and-go lifestyle my condo offered made me feel younger. Five years later, when I was ready for the next step in my adventure, I sold that property and headed off on a nomadic journey.

The moral of the story? When our lives change, we might as well change accordingly.

Staying Out of the Red

While I'm on the subject of change, I can't encourage you enough to wrap your mind around your new financial reality ASAP because it's very likely the partnered lifestyle you enjoyed for years is now beyond your means. If you're still hung up on the idea that money's complicated, snap out of it. Managing an ordinary budget is plain common sense. Of course, if you have money in capital amounts, you need an advisor.

As dull as it sounds, I recommend getting down to the nitty-gritty of tracking your moolah. Like exercise, it starts off a bit rough and later gets addictive. Dive into those bank statements, credit card statements, and cash receipts. Keep a spreadsheet, an old-fashioned ledger, or download an app—whatever it takes to know where your money is going.

You may be stunned to see how much money you're squandering once you review your spending habits with a fine-tooth comb. I got over my penchant for Starbucks when receipts showed my wallet taking more hits than a piñata at a children's party.

We all have spending quirks, and indulging a few occasionally can be great for our morale. But I suggest you keep your splurges small until you have your finger on your financial pulse. Be intentional and set aside a modest budget for your whims. An occasional spa pedicure, fresh bouquet, or something just as frivolous can be worth the price if you don't overdo it. Some forms of economizing will delight you. Others won't. I have well-dressed friends who adore thrift shopping. Not my cup of tea.

Meanwhile, my tastes in food are simpler and cheaper than my foodie friends could ever enjoy. Ladies, penny-pinching should be a game, not a punishment. Choose the spending and saving quirks that suit you best and have fun with them. As the late retail genius Richard Gump famously said, "Good taste costs no more." The more you cultivate your taste, the more chic you can be without breaking the bank.

Now, let's talk wheels. A car isn't an investment; it's a money pit. So get those car costs in check. A good rule of thumb is to keep your car payment down to no more than 15% of your net monthly income. You might also consider whether you really need that vehicle in the first place. For the past few years, I've found that living in walkable cities, sans car, fattened my piggy bank while toning my legs.

Starting over successfully is like a fabulous makeover—it takes a lot of thought, self-examination, and attitude! Don't settle for ho-hum now that you have this fresh opportunity to create something stunning!

Exercise 12: Remove & Replace

A couple of years after my divorce, I was so short of money I could hear my wallet echo when I opened it. By blessing, I landed a side gig as a heating and air unit recall repair technician. Oh, the glamour!

I could do the job because it required nothing more than the ability to operate an electric screwdriver. You see, in today's world of instant everything, many repairs are just a game of "remove and replace." Take out the defective part and pop in one that works. Easy peasy.

With that concept in mind, suppose you could rebuild your life with a bit of reverse engineering? You might get a dash of new insight and amaze yourself at how much better things work. Think of it as a DIY project for your soul, Ladies. Out with the obsolete, in with the new, Voila!. . and keep the rhinestone-studded safety goggles handy!

- Where are you now geographically?
- What brought you there?
- Are you happy there, or do you want to make a change? Explain.
- Where are you now, professionally?
- What brought you there?
- Are you happy, or do you want to make a change? Explain.
- Where are you now in terms of hobbies, activities, and friends?
- What brought you there?
- Are you happy, or do you want to make a change? Explain.

Exercise 13: Gratitude Remix

EMILY: "Does anyone ever realize life while
they live it...every, every minute?
STAGE MANAGER: No. Saints and poets maybe...they do some."
—FROM *OUR TOWN* BY THORNTON WILDER

Ladies, let's take a trip down memory lane. Can you recall a time when fate threw you a curveball, and your hopes were dashed? You were disappointed, crushed, and ready to toss in the towel, and then—surprise!—life handed you something even better!

It could have been...

- A job you didn't get.
- A loan you weren't approved for.
- A relationship that didn't work out.
- A college that didn't accept you.
- . . . Or any number of other things.

Can you think of some good things in your life that wouldn't be possible if you were still with your partner?

17

Your Super-Duper Subconscious

I hope you're still with me, Ladies because I've got a juicy piece of brainy gossip that'll knock your socks off! Picture this: Our subconscious mind, the unsung hero of the gray matter gang, comprises a whopping 90-95% of our brainpower. That's right, that backstage brainiac is the real deal, orchestrating our body's complex functions and quietly directing most of our thoughts, memories, and emotions while we're blissfully unaware. This multitasking super genius is processing a staggering 500,000 times more intel than our conscious mind could ever handle. Think of your conscious mind as the ocean's surface and your subconscious as all that lies beneath. So often, the wisdom, knowledge, and ideas we need are already in our minds. We just need to let them bubble up.

We don't have direct access to this powerhouse—and thank goodness, because it's way too complicated for us to tinker with. But it never sleeps. It's always working in the background, 24/7, from birth until our final curtain call. It handles a massive amount of information and input via our five senses. So, while a lot of sensory input gets our attention, there's also a slew of input under the radar.

Our subconscious regulates our heartbeat, blood pressure, digestion, electrolyte levels, breathing, equilibrium, body temperature, healing, hair growth, and more—all the way down to a sub-cellular level. It's incredible when you realize this complex physical machine we call our body functions in harmony most of the time.

Thanks to our subconscious, we can do countless things, like walking, swallowing, and blinking, without giving them a thought. For example, did you know that standing up from a seated position requires our subconscious to coordinate more than 50 muscles precisely? So, let's give a round of applause to our subconscious, the ultimate behind-the-scenes superstar!

So, why am I bringing all of this up?

Because at this turning point, you need all the help you can get, and your subconscious mind is your secret weapon—but only if you learn to enlist it.

You see, we can imprint certain things on our subconscious through repetition. Have you ever done a task on autopilot? That's your clever subconscious picking up the pattern and taking charge. The same thing drives the muscle memory involved in learning a new dance step or manual skill.

Your recurring thoughts and actions are like little streams of water carving paths in the sand after a downpour. Just like water, your mind loves the path of least resistance. That's why some things become automatic, and why changing a deeply ingrained behavior can feel as tricky as rerouting a river.

But your subconscious isn't just a collection of functions; it's the vault where all your memories and emotions are stashed. As the psychiatrist and psychoanalyst Carl Jung said, "Until you make the unconscious conscious, it will direct your life, and you will call it fate."

Now, I'm not suggesting you get lost in an endless labyrinth of self-analysis. There's a razor-thin line between healthy introspection and unhealthy rumination. No one wants to be that person who is so self-involved they're both ineffective and unbearable to be around. My goal is for you to become self-aware, not self-obsessed. Overanalyzing every past disappointment and hurt can convince us that our problems are the center of the universe.

Instead, let's focus on what we can control—our self-talk. We need to be aware that our self-talk matters because the subconscious mind takes everything literally. It doesn't get sarcasm or joking self-deprecation; it can't tell the difference between what's real and what's merely a figment of the imagination. It's like a nosy neighbor who is always eavesdropping.

Don't believe me? Close your eyes and picture this: you're holding a bright yellow lemon, its rich color practically glowing in your hand. You slice it open, and juice drips onto the cutting board while its tangy, citrus scent fills the air. Now, imagine biting into that lemon. Your teeth sink into its tart, juicy flesh, and the sourness makes you pucker.

If you fully commit to this thought, your mouth will start

watering, even though there's no lemon in sight. This phenomenon showcases the immense power of your subconscious mind. Just by visualizing and focusing on the sensory details, your brain triggers a physical response. Thinking about things that make us angry raises our adrenaline. Having a sexual fantasy arouses us physically. In short, our subconscious pulls the strings that cause reactions to what we feed it.

But unlike our conscious minds, the subconscious has no ego. It won't analyze or argue. That gives it the potential to be a compliant and extremely helpful servant, but only if we use it properly.

Three Suggestions to Harness Your Subconscious Power:

1. **Say positive things about yourself.** Remember, your subconscious takes everything literally, so don't say anything you don't want to become your reality. Forgot your umbrella when it's raining? Don't say, "I always forget my umbrella," because your subconscious will think it's supposed to make that accurate. Instead, say, "I usually remember my umbrella." This tiny difference in language can make a world of difference. Forgot a name when you're telling a story? Don't say, "I forgot." Say, "It'll come to me." Instead of saying, "I need to lose weight," say, "I'm becoming more health conscious." You get the idea!

2. **Learn to listen to and trust your intuition.** The word *intuition* is a gem—it means being taught (tuition) from within. In addition to intuition, women our age have layers of learning, and so our "Aha!" moments and "Oh no!" reactions merit our attention. Often, a series of small revelations can save us from disaster and set us on the right path. So whenever you

have a hunch, pause and consider it instead of just brushing it off.

3. **When you're uncertain about something, release it to your subconscious and move on.** Literally say, "I'm releasing that problem to my subconscious." Nine times out of ten, a solution will naturally emerge in your conscious mind in a matter of hours. Another trick? Ask yourself a question before you go to sleep. There's a good chance you'll wake up with the answer at the forefront of your mind.

Embrace the mystery, trust the process, and remember—sometimes it's perfectly okay to let that mental maestro handle the complexities while we enjoy the performance from the front row.

III

Hit Your Stride

"As you start to walk on the way . . . the way appears."
—RUMI

A backpacker came across an old man working in an apple orchard beside a country road. She stopped walking and called out, "Excuse me, Sir. How long will it take me to get to the next town?"

The old man looked down at her from his ladder for a moment, then replied, "I can't tell."

Slightly annoyed, she strode away.

When she had gone about twenty steps, the old man shouted after her, "About half an hour."

The backpacker turned around and said, "Why didn't you say so when I asked?"

"Because," the old man said, "I didn't know how fast you were walking."

Likewise, I can't predict how long your life transformation will take, but I can offer some practical tools and advice to help you move forward efficiently . . . stay tuned.

18

Learn to Discern

Ladies, you've got places to be, dreams to conquer, and no time for the little nuisances that try to trip you up along the way. Take charge of your destiny because luck favors the bold, and why leave it to chance when you can whip up your own good fortune? It's like baking a cake—sure, you could wing it and hope it rises, but doesn't it make more sense to follow a recipe?

At this stage in life, competence is our currency, and sophistication is our calling card. We may not be spring chickens, but we've got style, grace, capabilities, and a killer sense of self. Who needs fluffy feathers when you've got the whole henhouse of experience? A calm, collected woman ages like a timeless work of art. But letting chaos in mars the picture. So honor your good habits like they're celebrities at the *Golden Globes*, and watch as your luck turns from ordinary to extraordinary.

Here are three magic "Learn to Discern" caveats that will help improve your luck:

1. Learn to Discern: The difference between procrastination and self-care.
Ladies, our modern world seems to be obsessed with "self-care." It's all well and good until you look a little closer and realize that the self-care industry has taken a wild ride into Crazytown. It's become a high-stakes game of "who can spend more?" in an endless cycle of buying more stuff. I mean, there's a product for everything now. Lip masks, hair masks, neck masks, décolletage masks, face masks, eye masks, foot masks . . . .If there's a body part, there's a mask for it. It's like a Halloween costume party in your bathroom every night! A little self-care is great, but when every day's a spa day at Procrastination Resort, it's time to return to reality.

And there's no good reason to spend an entire morning meditating about how you're going to tackle your tasks while your deadline gathers dust, getting elbow-deep in a culinary masterpiece because you need healthy food to fuel your productivity, or playing the "I need a mental health day" card so you can binge-watch your favorite shows. It's like ordering a Diet Coke with a triple cheeseburger and fries—you're not fooling anyone!

The longer we delay, the more daunting our work becomes, and before we know it, we're drowning in a sea of laziness and panic. So, let's pair self-care with common sense and not let it become the ultimate excuse for procrastination. Balance, Ladies, balance!

2. Learn to Discern: A real vs a false promise to yourself.
Self-confidence starts with trusting yourself. We've all been through days when the world was about as reliable as a cheap

umbrella in a thunderstorm. That's why you need to be your own umbrella. Think of self-trust as a sturdy, well-built bridge to your best life—strong, reliable, and able to withstand any storm. Every time you keep a promise to yourself, it's like reinforcing that bridge with another solid beam. On that note, don't make a promise to yourself unless you mean it. If you tell yourself you'll hit the gym after work and end up at Happy Hour instead, you just stood yourself up. You wouldn't trust a flake who always canceled at the last minute, right? So treat your commitments to yourself like V.I.P. tickets to the hottest show in town. When you say you're going to do something, do it—no ifs, ands, buts, or maybe laters and build rock-solid self-confidence one honored promise at a time.

3. Learn to Discern quick decisions vs impulsive ones.
This section of the book wouldn't be complete without diving into the delightful chaos of decision-making. Hold on tight because we're about to take a spin through a whirlwind of choices and a tornado of temptations.

We've all made snap decisions like committing to plans we couldn't care less about, letting the saleswoman at the cosmetic counter fill our shopping bag with products like we're in a supermarket sweep, or whipping out a credit card for . . . . say, a Max Mara cocktail dress. You know you'll hardly wear it, but the fashion devil is whispering sweet nothings in your ear. And how about the smooth-talking charmer trying to take you back to his place at the end of the first date? Oh, Honey. He's laying it on thicker than a drag queen's makeup! Or the slick salesman pushing you to trade in your car for the latest model while he's practically rubbing his hands together like a cartoon villain.

Granted, we must be decisive, but let's not cave under

pressure. Decision-making should be more like fine dining than fast food. Study the menu—including the prices, consider the options, and place your order in a comfortable amount of time. Don't let anyone rush you into a McDecision!

Remember, Ladies, you're not a feather in the wind or a jelly doughnut in the hands of a toddler. When the world twists your arm, stand firm and channel your inner diva. This is *your* life, not anyone else's!

19
Consistency Is Queen

*"The key is not to prioritize what's on your
schedule, but to schedule your priorities."*
—STEPHEN COVEY

Don't get me wrong, Ladies. I'm not saying you should turn into a robot with a rigid routine. Routines are powerful, and a semblance of routine gives your life a solid foundation, but it's a delicate balance. That's why I don't go along with the multitude of *YouTube* influencers and other trendy self-help gurus who advise you to get up at 5 a.m., have elaborate morning rituals, or follow any other "one size fits all" lifestyle prescription.

We all fare better when we're in tune with our bodies and minds. It's all about finding what works best for you and *consistently* sticking to it.

Take a page from Mark Twain's book—literally. The man spent mornings in bed writing while puffing a cigar. Jackie Kennedy threw stodgy routines out the window and set her own stylish pace. And how about Albert Einstein? He kept odd hours and followed his own quirky schedule, showing that genius operates on its own time. But these three had one thing in common: They were consistent when it came to doing what mattered most.

So, here are my top tips for all you fierce femmes who want your productivity to soar like a champagne cork on New Year's Eve.

I. Tune Into Your Natural Body Clock.

Let's delve into the art and science of working smarter, not harder. Past research suggests that 40%-70% of your circadian rhythm, or body clock, is genetically determined. Some scientists argue that this genetic predisposition stems from our communal roots as humans—back in the prehistoric days when part of the tribe was always on watch while others caught some Z's.

They say it's likely these instincts still influence us today.

Age also plays a role; if you find early mornings easier now than you did in your teen years, thank the calendar!

Bottom line: To unlock your happiest, healthiest, and most successful self, do what you can to sync up with your body's natural rhythms. Identify when you're firing on all cylinders—mentally and physically—and tackle those tasks that demand your A-game during those peak times. Trust me, once you're in sync, you'll be an unstoppable force!

2. Prep Like a Pro.

Ask any successful person their secret weapon; if they're honest, they'll say it's all in the prep game. The beauty of this strategy? It's an equal-opportunity advantage—no special skills required. So, here's the deal: plan your morning the night before. Know what you'll eat for breakfast, choose your clothes, and map out that next day's priorities like a boss. Morning clarity can set your whole day. While everyone else is still trying to find their other shoe and hunting for their keys, you'll already be miles ahead!

3. Give Yourself Ample Time in A.M.

Try to get up at least two hours before you need to be anywhere. That way, you'll glide through your morning like a swan on a serene lake instead of rushing in circles like a headless chicken. That extra time means you can enjoy breakfast, take a look at the news, and get your head in the game. In today's hectic world, showing up with an air of cool, calm, and collected confidence will give you an elegant, authoritative air and an unforgettable vibe.

4. Have a Zero-Tolerance Policy for Clutter.

Clutter is like that unwanted guest who never leaves and always spills something on your carpet. Believe me, Ladies, you'll be healthier, happier, and more together if you embrace a zero-tolerance policy for messes in every nook and cranny of your life. A clutter-free lifestyle isn't just about tidiness; it's about using your resources wisely and reclaiming your space, sanity, and style. Once you discover the magic of stellar organization, you'll wonder how you ever lived without it. And hey, you might even discover those reading glasses weren't really stolen by gremlins after all!

5. Practice Purse Intervention.

Speaking of banishing clutter, every night, empty that handbag into an attractive basket. I mean, dump it *all* out and sort through the chaos. The next day, choose a purse and fill it only with the essentials. This will keep you feeling sleek and chic instead of muddled. You're too gorgeous to be weighed down by a bag full of mayhem, and there's nothing cool and attractive about rummaging around in your purse like you're on a scavenger hunt. Once you embrace the art of a minimally and perfectly packed bag, your shoulders will thank you, your style will shine, and you'll be ready to take on the world.

6. Write Things Down.

Whether it's that million-dollar idea or just a reminder to grab laundry detergent, don't let that thought tumble into the black hole of forgetfulness. Jot it down. Modern life can feel like herding a bunch of cats on a sugar high—chaotic, unpredictable, and a bit scratchy. Our frazzled brains can only juggle so much. You'll keep your mind as clear as a polished diamond by writing things down. Think of it as giving yourself a first-class ticket to the fabulous world of high productivity. Cheers to being your own personal assistant!

7. Break Big Jobs into Smaller Tasks.

Got a daunting project? Chop that beast into bite-sized bits. Picture a mountain of dirty dishes. Start with the silverware— bam! Small victory. Move on to the glassware—another triumph! Frequent wins are a great motivator, and by slicing and dicing your tasks, you'll rack up wins faster than a slot machine hitting jackpots. It's the most practical way to turn "ugh" into "heck yeah!" keeping your energy up and your stress down.

8. If you don't want to do something, commit to only 5 minutes.

That's right, just five measly minutes. It's like dipping your toe into chilly water—unpleasant at first, but soon, you'll be up to your ankles. And before you know it, you'll be splashing around like a dolphin at a pool party. Ladies, you can't be unstoppable unless you start, and remember, even the smallest splash makes waves. So, grab those five minutes and make a splash in the sea of productivity!

9. Adopt a Professional Mindset.

Tackle your dreams, goals, and projects as if you're working for the most demanding boss in town—none of that scatterbrained, self-indulgent nonsense. And focus on just 2-3 real goals per quarter. Any more, and you'll be spread thinner than a slice of prosciutto at *Eataly*. Set deadlines and hold yourself accountable. Success doesn't come from winging it, Ladies—it comes from careful planning!

10. Pace Yourself.

Forget about sprinting—it's all about mastering this marathon with finesse. No more rollercoaster energy; let's aim for steady, consistent progress with a dash of grace and a dollop of pizzazz. For example, imagine tackling your prospect list like a pro. Instead of burning out after a day, set a sustainable goal—like making 20 daily phone calls. By year's end, you'll have made over 5,000 calls without breaking a sweat. Stay steady, and you'll conquer mountains without having to stop for a double espresso!

11. BUSY is a Four-Letter Word.

Oh, my glamorous Ladies, can we talk about this cult of busyness that's taken over? Ask someone how they're doing these days, and they'll likely sigh heavily and drop the word "busy" as if it's a badge of honor they didn't sign up for. Not a good look.

Being constantly swamped screams unfocused priorities, poor organization, and chronic escapism. It's like trying to whip up a soufflé while juggling eggs—potentially messy, not cute.

Instead, aim to be focused, intentional, selective, and oh-so-effective. Know your purpose, zero in on your priorities, and watch the distractions fade away like yesterday's fads. And let's give a standing ovation to the power of "No"—embrace it and say goodbye to guilt trips. At this fabulous turning point, anything that doesn't vibe with your dreams, vision, or priorities can see itself out. Thank you!

So, instead of rushing off to the next thing you couldn't care less about, take a breather, recharge, and focus on what truly lights up your life. Because in the grand finale, it's not about how busy you are—it's about how well you live your life.

12. Schedule offline time for your most creative tasks.
Protect this time like it's a winning lottery ticket. Picture this: no phone ringing, no emails pinging, no doorbell dinging, no radio singing, and no T.V. or internet zinging. The world can wait; your brilliance can't.

Whether it's a couple of hours every other day or a sacred block of time once a week, hold it inviolate, Ladies. You'll be amazed at how this dedicated offline time fuels your creativity and sparks your imagination like nothing else. It's like giving your brain a spa day—pure bliss and rejuvenation!

Remember: You can't do big things if you keep getting distracted by small things. Prioritize your goals and dreams like a NASA flight director overseeing a rocket launch.

Exercise 14: Assess Your Effort

*"The difference between those that succeed and those
that fail is those that succeeded tried."*
—MARK TWAIN

Are you trying or pretending to try?

Be honest. In the last three months, how often have you found
yourself. . . .

- Talking about what you're going to do over and over with-
  out taking any steps?
  Never / Rarely / From time to time / Regularly / Often
- Opting out of something, thinking, "It's a rigged game,
  so I'm not going to play"?
  Never / Rarely / From time to time / Regularly / Often
- Giving yourself credit for your potential instead of what
  you've actually done?
  Never / Rarely / From time to time / Regularly / Often
- Telling yourself you'll binge eat, drink too much, buy
  something extravagant on credit, procrastinate for an
  entire day, "One last time"?
  Never / Rarely / From time to time / Regularly / Often
- Telling yourself, "I'll do better next time," without im-
  plementing a strategy and taking those first steps?
  Never / Rarely / From time to time / Regularly / Often

Look over your answers.

They'll give you a good indication of whether you're not really
trying or just pretending to try.

If you're pretending to try, you can do better, and you know it.

20

Navigate Your Career Path

"Surround yourself with people who
do what you want to do,
and eventually, you'll wake up to find
yourself doing the same."
—JUSTIN KAN

If you're content with where you are professionally or are happily retired with no desire ever to work again, this chapter isn't for you. Everyone else, let's cut through the noise and get real—especially if life has thrown you a curveball and you're suddenly in the hustle to provide for yourself.

Whether you're not working and haven't worked for a while or are working but need more income, you might have to get your nose out of the air about lower-level jobs and side hustles. Getting over my snobbishness was, far and away, one of the best choices I ever made.

What you need right now is M.O.N.E.Y.

You don't need to slide further into debt or get that unemployed vibe about you. No matter where you start, you'll feel better if you have to get up, clean up, and show up.

I still typically work six days a week, plus a few evenings, and guess what? I'd rather have paychecks to cash than time on my hands. Once you get used to it, you might feel the same way.

Of course, money isn't the whole shebang. Over the long haul, you also need that emotional spark from your work. It's a three-part harmony: the job, the paycheck, and your heart should all sing from the same piece of music as much as possible.

If you're starting over with no career or are determined to make a career change, seek the help or inspiration you need to find a solid direction. You wouldn't tell your G.P.S. to take you "someplace nice," so don't do the equivalent with your career. Without an inspired goal, you're just another face in the crowd of uninspired souls.

Of course, if your finances were turned on their head, we're talking shelter, not self-actualization right now. Find a survival job, ideally one with some benefits, whether it thrills you or not—start cashing those paychecks while you plot and plan to get the skills, inspiration, and body of work you need to succeed.

Every woman at a turning point like ours should dedicate herself to finding work that sets her soul on fire. You're too unique to numb your mind and punch a clock like an automaton for the rest of your productive life. Imagine a place where everyone is radiant with inspiration. That's the vibe I want you to gravitate to and become a part of. We were put on this earth to shine; living inspired is our birthright. So, channel your inner Da Vinci, Steve Jobs, or Oprah and let that creative energy flow.

Sure, getting older comes with its own set of career challenges. But guess what? You're not alone in this rodeo. So, put on your networking hat and start building those connections. (If the thought of Networking intimidates you. Don't worry. There's a whole chapter on it coming up soon.) Meanwhile, whether it's joining a professional organization, cozying up to industry veterans, going to the business center in your local library to research free resources, attending a career fair, going to an employment agency, or seeking a career coach, surround yourself with people and information that can lift you higher. If you have to do some homework to find where those people hang out, do it.

Learn the current standard for a resume in the industry you want to join and get one together. The standards for resumes are ever-evolving, so don't just update the one you used last. Look at job postings, too, and make sure you write your resume with the same keywords. I'm not talking about lying. I'm talking about meticulous wording. Put some real thought into what value you can bring to a business or client. If you need help with your resume, ask a qualified friend, hire a professional, or use a resume-building tool.

Get some cards made, even if all you can have on them is your name, phone number, and email; put them in your purse and start showing up. It may be as simple as joining your local Toastmasters, Rotary, or Lyons Club, attending meetups and mixers, going to career fairs, getting back in touch with old friends and former coworkers, volunteering, and rubbing more elbows in the places you already frequent. Leave no stone unturned, and don't be shy about mentioning your skills and intended direction.

When it comes to obstacles like ageism and sexism, we've all faced them. Here's the bottom line: complaining won't pay the bills. All you can do is find something you want so badly you can taste it, lace up your boots, and march forward with the resolve to let nothing—absolutely nothing—stand in your way.

If the corporate world isn't making you an offer, consider applying to small businesses owned by people close to your age. Find niches where age adds authority. And when you interview, don't act like a fuddy-duddy or a new broom that will burst in and try to sweep everything into her (possibly outdated) concept of a great workplace.

Even though you'll have to be diplomatic and may have to start small, always think like a leader.

My friend, Deborah, was single several years ago with two teenage daughters at home. She got a job answering the phone at a dental office, quickly learned all she could, and, in time, marshaled social media and email to reach out to as many other dental office administrators in her community as she could find. From there, she formed an informal professional association that met in a restaurant one evening a month. They ate, drank, shared experiences and ideas, and devised ways to run their offices more smoothly. Those meetings were so successful that her boss and other local dental offices soon acknowledged the group and provided a budget for their get-togethers. Deborah was also promoted. She turned a ho-hum job into a career thanks to her brainpower, great attitude, and determination. Whenever you're given a small opportunity, think outside the box and see if you can turn it into something bigger.

If working for someone else isn't your bag, consider starting your own business. Everyone has some skills people will pay for. Acquire some basic business knowledge and a little tech savvy because you'll need those skills for promotion, administration, and outreach. It might be best to start by getting a basic job in a business like the one you want to open to learn all you can.

If you're not monetized (I wasn't when I started my business, *Savvy Civility*), consider a service business you can start with little to no overhead. If you need help, visit the small business center of your public library and the Small Business Association (S.B.A.) website to see what they have to offer. Do a *Google* search and see what grants are available. While you're at it, look into SCORE. This organization is staffed by retired professionals who share their business knowledge for free. And again, write down your ideas. Always.

If you feel a little rudderless because you're still rediscovering yourself career-wise, embrace this opportunity to experiment and explore. Dive into the gig economy, or find a "fun" job—even if it's on the side. The sky's the limit if you use your imagination. (Don't worry; there's a chapter on Creativity further along in the book.)

So, Ladies, don't just sit there—get creative, get bold, and get moving. Your next big success might be just one idea or one connection away!

Last but certainly not least, it's never too late to learn. Whether updating your resume or mastering a new skill, seize every opportunity to grow and evolve. Today's world offers some great free and low-cost opportunities to pick up skills and earn certifications online, so get Googling!

Success is calling. Get ready, willing, and able to answer.

Remember: If you want to find a new career path later in life, you may have to do some off-roading.

Exercise 15: Navigate Your Career Path

If you feel intimidated by the prospect of entering the workforce, changing your line of work, or adding an income source, it's time to sort yourself out.

Whatever you do, don't undervalue any of your experience. You've likely got a treasure trove of talents, skills, and knowledge, but nobody will value it unless you do. Believe me, your experience is gold, and it's time to cash in!

- List everything you've ever been paid to do and what skills those jobs require.
- List all the volunteer positions you've ever held and what skills they require.
- What compliments have you received about your skills and abilities?
- Are there any recurring themes to those compliments?
- List the things you know you're exceptionally good at. Those are your God-given gifts. It doesn't matter if they're hobbies.
- Look over your lists. Where does your experience intersect with your gifts?
- How can you bring more value to others using your gifts?
- Make an open-ended list of business, freelance, and employment ideas, or consider doing what I did and write a new idea on each index card.

Chances are some of those ideas will incorporate your existing skills, while others may require you to up-skill. If you need new or updated skills, list them and find the most efficient, effective, and affordable way to acquire them. If you need help figuring out where to start, ask a few pros who know the ropes. At first, your gift may only be a hobby, but if you're creative, bold, and determined, you can probably find a way to make it pay.

- Identify a role model or mentor whose career path you admire.
- What skills and qualities do they have that you would like to develop?
- How have they navigated their career to leverage their skills?
- What can you learn from their experiences to apply to your career journey?

Remember, Ladies, you're not just making a comeback—you're unleashing your inner dynamo! So, swing open those doors and let the world know there's no stopping you now!

21

Build Your Network

*"You can't stay in your corner of the forest
waiting for others to come to you.
You have to go to them sometimes."*
—A. A. MILNE

Now, Ladies, one of the best things about building your new life is that you're destined to meet new people. However, creating a professional network is a more deliberate process that's about much more than collecting business cards and *LinkedIn* connections. It's about curating a circle of individuals you honestly like and respect who'll inspire, lift you higher and cheer you on.

Anyone can become a SuperNetworker! Here's How:

1. **Know Your Goals.** Knowing your goals will help you identify the kind of people you need in your professional

network. It's like shopping for shoes—you wouldn't buy ballet flats for a hiking trip, right?

2. **Be Authentic.** Authenticity is your best accessory. People are drawn to genuine personalities. So be yourself and stand out in a sea of sameness. Never forget that there's only one you, and *that's* your superpower.

3. **Attend Industry Events.** Get yourself out there. Attend industry conferences, seminars, workshops, and networking events. These places are gold mines for meeting like-minded professionals. And don't just stand in the corner observing—mingle! Start conversations, ask questions, and show genuine interest in others.

4. **Leverage Social Media.** Social media isn't just for posting selfies and cat videos. Platforms like *LinkedIn*, *Twitter*, *Instagram*, *TikTok*, and *YouTube* can be powerful tools for building your professional network. So share your achievements, insights, and industry news. Engage with posts from others in your field. Slide into D.M.s with a purpose. Show that you're knowledgeable and involved.

5. **Be a Connector.** One of the best ways to build a network is to be a connector. Introduce people who could benefit from knowing each other. When you help others build their networks, they're more likely to help you build yours. Plus, it shows that you're a thoughtful, generous person—which you *are*!

Now that you've started building a network, let's talk about keeping it strong and vibrant. Networks require regular care and attention.

1. **Stay in Touch.** A friendly email, a comment on their

latest post, or a coffee catch-up every now and then works wonders.

2. **Offer Value.** Share valuable information, offer help when you can, and celebrate other people's successes.

3. **Attend Follow-Up Events.** Keep showing up. If there are regular events or meetings in your industry, make a habit of attending. This consistency shows that you're committed and serious about your career. Plus, it gives you more opportunities to deepen relationships and meet new people.

4. **Be Genuinely Interested.** Ask questions, remember details about people, and bring those details up in conversations. This shows that you care and that you're invested in the relationship. (It doesn't hurt to jot down a few notes on the people you meet after the event.)

5. **Express Gratitude.** If someone helps you out, thank them. If they give you advice, let them know how it helped you. A little appreciation goes a long way. And who doesn't love a thank you note or a shoutout?

6. **Be Resilient.** Building a network takes time and effort. Don't get discouraged if you don't see immediate results. Keep at it, stay positive, and remember that every connection you make is a step toward your goal.

7. **Have Fun.** Networking shouldn't be a chore. If you're interested in achieving your goals, you'll enjoy meeting new people, learning new things, and growing your circle. When you're having fun, it shows—and people are naturally drawn to positive, vibrant women. By the same token, if most of the people you're meeting leave you cold, you might be in the wrong industry. But no matter what industry you're in, choose your soirees wisely. You can't

afford to run with people whose idea of a professional event involves heavy drinking, gossip, flirting galore, and staggering into an Uber at the crack of dawn. And, of course, steer clear of those who expect you to break the bank to keep up with their lifestyle.

Anyone can build a terrific circle of professional connections. Like so many things, it's all in the approach. Now, go out there and work your magic!

Remember: "Don't walk through the world looking for evidence that you don't belong, because you will always find it."—Brené Brown.

22
Return to Romance

"When you find love later in life
you do it with all the wisdom of knowing heartbreak,
and all the peace of knowing who you are."
—Kerry Spencer

'm a straight cisgender woman, so I'm writing this chapter with those pronouns, but that doesn't mean I'm disregarding the rest of the world. Aside from that, anyone who wants "No Strings," casual, hedonistic flings, can skip this chapter. Sexual opportunities abound for women of all ages. You won't have to look very far if that's all you want.

On the other hand, as a true romantic, I wrote this chapter for Ladies looking for something deep and lasting. To be sure, in today's world, that old-fashioned path is often fraught with obstacles. The dating landscape has undergone quite a transformation since our last stint in Singledom. I don't know about you, but when I made my first foray, I felt like I was navigating a foreign bazaar with a pocketful of exotic currencies. And don't even get me started on the bewildering new lexicon of romance—swiping, breadcrumbing, ghosting, pocketing, situationships, and other post-modern games that are enough to make us sometimes consider running off to join the nearest convent or circus! (If those terms leave you boggled, don't worry; there'll be more on them later.)

I'll never forget a conversation with a shopkeeper in Taos, New Mexico, shortly after my marriage fell apart in 2014. "I meet so many awesome women whose partners have left them," she said. "I can't help but wonder, where are the matches for those women?"

A decade later, I have to admit that I often wonder the same thing. These days, a lot of men behave like boys in grownup bodies. (And don't get me started on that Peter Pan syndrome.)

The challenges I've encountered have been with the "Three C's"—Compatibility, Character, and Commitment. Nowadays, so many men excel at pretending that finding a genuine one is like searching for a diamond in a sea of cubic zirconias.

Oh, and by the way, if you're newly alone, brace yourself. Once word gets around, you may be surprised by the number of men coming out of the woodwork. Some may have always fancied you; some may want to be your knight in shining armor, and others may think your vulnerability will make you easy to manipulate. Keep your cool, and don't read too much into their advances. If there's a right man among them, he'll understand the importance of taking things slow while you adjust to the many significant changes in your life.

Meanwhile, modern society and some of our well-meaning friends would have us diving into romantic encounters for the sheer thrill of it—flitting in and out of beds like butterflies on a nectar binge, utterly unfazed by the transient nature of it all. Now, I'm not here to judge. If that's what you want, go for it. But at least guard your heart and practice personal safety as well as safe sex.

For those of us who crave more than a quick fling, finding a partner will be a longer, more intentional process. Our confidence may have taken a blow from past betrayals and/or oppressive partners. But reclaiming our mojo is our responsibility because, Ladies if we don't seize the reins of our romantic destiny, who will?

Feeling Confident and Desirable

Getting ready for an encore appearance on the romantic stage requires self-assurance, self-awareness, and moxie. It might also take a bit of proactive self-improvement. If the thought of baring it all turns your stomach into knots, consider embarking on a journey of diet, exercise, and maybe even some counseling to help you get your groove back.

For better or worse, men are known to be creatures of sight. They notice more than they let on. That said, if there are any available men in your orbit, you can be sure they'll notice you—especially if you're taking care of yourself, dressing attractively, and generally playing your cards right.

Contrary to the doomsayers who insist that every man wants a 19-year-old porn star, we actually have a lot of control over our sex appeal. Quality men are drawn to a woman's character, unique vibe, grace under pressure, sophistication, and zest for life. And eloquence? Oh, Ladies, well-spoken heartfelt words can weave a spell as enchanting as any love potion.

So once you feel you're, say, 75% ready to date, I think it

makes sense to tastefully spread the word. If your friends, colleagues, kinfolk, and even that neighborhood barista who makes your coffee just right, all know you'd like to meet someone, one of them might just play Cupid and introduce you to the man of your dreams.

While you're at it, try putting yourself in what the military calls "target-rich zones" where you're likely to meet men. Whether your ideal man is an athletic Adonis, an intellectual scholar, a civic-minded hero, a sports fan, an artistic soul, a business maverick, or any other type, seek out events and locales where your type of man is most likely to be found. Delve into volunteering, get a new part-time gig, enroll in a class, join a club, go to meetups—the list goes on and on. Say "Yes" to invitations to parties. Nothing will happen if you just stay home.

Get in the habit of breaking the ice.

I know it may sound old-fashioned, but I still believe in charming encounters. I hope you believe in them, too. Eye contact, a dazzling smile, and deliberate proximity can work wonders in a safe social setting. Even so, you still have to notice attractive men and speak to them. You don't have to be witty, just pleasant and proactive. Our great-grandmothers accidentally dropped their white lace hankies near dashing men, hoping they'd pick them up and break the ice. Surely, we can be just as courageous. Nothing you say needs to be more than a subtle invitation for them to start a conversation. It's not Rocket Science, Ladies! How about . . .

- "I love your style. Where did you get that jacket?"
- "Do you have a pen I could borrow for a second?"
- "My GPS is acting up. Do you know how to get to _______?"

- "Could you please take a quick photo of me?"
- "I'm deciding between these two flavors. Which one do you like?"
- "Could you please help me reach that item on the top shelf?"
- "Your dog is adorable! Can I pet him?"
- "Would you mind holding this for a second while I get my keys?"
- "I'm debating between these two sweaters. Which color do you think looks best?"
- "Can you please hand me the catsup?"
- "My phone is about to die. Would you be willing to lend me a charger for a few minutes?"
- "Do you know which bus/train I should take to get to __________?" etcetera, etcetera. . . . Simple as that.

He'll keep the conversation going if he likes you, and he's even a smidgen gregarious. If he's not interested, he'll let it fizzle out. No harm done.

If you see a man you like, leverage proximity. If you're in an art gallery, for example, walk over and look at the painting he's looking at. Eventually, one of you will say something.

On days when you're feeling bold, full of fun, and fancy-free, take a conversation piece for a spin and see how many men will break the ice. For example, read a book with an eye-catching cover in a coffee shop or sport an unusual hat or graphic t-shirt that's likely to spark conversation. I picked up a hardcover book of Groucho Marx's letters a few years ago—not as a man trap, but because I knew I'd enjoy it. One afternoon, I was reading that book in a coffee shop, and over the course of about two hours, three nice, age-appropriate men came up and spoke to me because Groucho's picture caught their eye and gave them a little incentive to say, "Hello."

Now, if you've been married or partnered for years, you'll probably have to get back in the habit of noticing men, let alone breaking the ice. Time to get with it—you don't want to be a shameless flirt, but you do need to get some game.

Online Dating

I think meeting men online is challenging, though many women will tell you the opposite. Packaging myself with a bio and photos makes me feel a little like a candy bar or a bottle of barbecue sauce in an ad. And then, as the responses come in, I feel strange about making split-second swiping decisions based on a photo. But again, a lot of women swear by the apps.

Now, please be aware that a lot of men primarily use dating apps to look for sex, money, or other opportunities instead of relationships. Also, be aware that the companies that own the apps throw in some fake profiles—complete with AI chatbot—to keep people hooked, optimistic, and willing to upgrade their accounts. So be careful and, dare I say, even skeptical while still knowing you might have great luck. Your ideal match might be just a click away.

Your Dating App Photos

The *New York Times* bestselling author and dating guru Matthew Hussey says your first photo should be a good, clear, current close-up. Your profile pic will make a better first impression if you have a pleasant, vivacious smile. If you can afford to have your picture taken professionally, so much the better. But please don't go overboard with the filters or Photoshopping. No man wants to wonder if a cartoon character might be catfishing him.

Include a flattering, full-length photo somewhere in your profile, too. Also, post quality images that show various sides of your personality—dressy, businesslike, casual, outdoorsy, etc.

Genuine snapshots of you in different situations are far more effective than a series of selfies. But please, Ladies, no group photos. Men are on the dating app to see you, not to play *Where's Waldo?*

Don't post anything overly provocative. We're going for alluring, not desperate. And please, for your safety, only use photos that aren't anywhere else online. The last thing you need is some maniac doing a reverse image lookup and finding out where you work or live—unless you aspire to have your story in a true crime documentary. When you upload your photos, make sure they're clear and complete without any weird distortion. Be meticulous because you only have a split second to make a killer first impression, and after all, you're a catch!

Your Dating App Profile

Keep your profile light and simple. No one's gets on a dating app to read *War and Peace*. Being too intense, lengthy, or complicated won't add to your appeal. Besides, why should anyone bother meeting you if they've already read your entire life story online? Be honest about your age and dating goals, but keep it breezy. Avoid the clichés like "long walks on the beach" (unless you're interested in dating a seagull), but don't try so hard to be unique that you sound like a carnival sideshow.

Remember, this is just a first impression, not an audition for a reality TV show. Keep it short, sweet, and irresistible—leave them wanting more! The best dating profiles spark curiosity, like the trailer for a great film.

First Connections

If you're going to reach out to a man on an app, don't just say, "Hi," make some effort. Use the man's name, say something original, and ask a fun question that will start a conversation.

If he asks for your phone number and you feel uncertain, tell him you'd prefer his. Let him sweat it out and wonder if you'll call. If you give him your number, tell him you prefer he calls you instead of texting. Here's why:

A lot of men juggle multiple text conversations like they're running an airport control tower. If he's sneaky, he can text you while another woman is sitting or even lying beside him. He can also copy and paste his charming "Good morning, Beautiful!" shtick to 50 women in less than a minute. He can't pull off those shenanigans with a phone call.

Besides, you need to hear his vocal inflections and manner of communication. You're never going to get to know a man through emojis. And if a man really likes you, he won't be indifferent to the sound of your voice.

If those early calls lead to some dates, you find yourselves in a relationship. Texting for logistics and quick check-ins is perfectly fine. But don't let texts set the standard of communication in the beginning. Insist on those phone calls and get to know the real man behind the screen!

Know Your Non-negotiables.

Consider what your non-negotiables are, and then ask yourself why. Are your dealbreakers based on principle, personal taste, or external pressures? At our age, external pressures should be discarded faster than an overripe avocado. Once you're confident about your non-negotiables, you'll be better positioned to listen and rule out incompatible prospects. Remember, Ladies, you're looking for a partner, not a project. That said, those early dates shouldn't feel like interrogations—unless you both have a fetish for that sort of thing.

First Dates

When it comes to first dates, simplicity is best. Instead of agonizing over what to wear, choose a stylish, flattering, and comfy outfit, and make it your first date uniform. The guys won't know, and it'll save you hours of wardrobe stress. Not only is your dating superhero costume always ready at a moment's notice, but it's also your reminder that the guy you're about to meet for the first time hasn't earned the privilege of special effort.

Opt for a short, casual date in a public place, and arrange your own transportation. Keep it brief, leaving room for a second date if there's mutual chemistry. Arrive on time, phone tucked away, order something without alcohol, and enjoy a little light, natural conversation. Avoid speaking in absolutes or asking hard questions. If your date says something you disagree with, don't argue. Keep your cool and ask why he holds that point of view. Remember, this is a brief date; you can sort out your thoughts and feelings later. Be candid and honest, but for heaven's sake, don't tell your life story or get intense. If he's inclined to do most of the talking on the first date, let him. It's a great way to gauge his personality and possibly even learn what skeletons are rattling around in his closet.

And Ladies, don't go in looking to spot trouble. Finding fault with every potential partner is a surefire recipe for ending up alone. If you spot red flags or dealbreakers during that first cup of coffee, don't overreact. Remember, it's just a first date. You never have to see him again if you don't want to. When in doubt, ask questions to make sure you understood what he said. If whatever he said or did is a dealbreaker, remember, there's no point in arguing or compromising your integrity. Bid a polite goodbye, leave gracefully, and let that be the end of it right there.

Even if he seems terrific and you like everything about him, hold your horses! Don't shower him with too much encouragement too soon. Salt and sugar look the same at a glance. So take your time to make sure he's as sweet as he seems.

First dates aren't for tooting your own horn.
Let your talents, independence, and successes speak for themselves in due time. Besides being crass, boasting is aggressive. And any man who deserves your attention won't measure your worth by your paycheck or status.

Let him pay for the first couple of dates.
I'm all for equality, and I know it's a two-way street, but Ladies, if you pull out your wallet too soon, you won't give the man a chance to step into the masculine role or demonstrate any generosity. Beyond that, if he can't buy you two plates of food without thinking you owe him money or sex, he doesn't have the level of *savoir-faire* you deserve. Once you get to know each other a little better, of course, you ought to pitch in according to your ability. After all, if you want a healthy relationship, you need to be a team player.

Don't Get in the Habit of Collecting these Red Flags—or worse yet, painting them green.
Some red flags are deal breakers. Others are questionable. The word questionable means just that: When in doubt, ask questions

about his words or behavior to make sure you understood him correctly.

Here's a partial list of things to watch out for—in no particular order:

- **Disrespectful Behavior:** Does he repeatedly interrupt you, talk over you, make belittling or inappropriate comments, openly ogle other women, or show a general lack of good manners?
- **Self-Centeredness:** Does he dominate the conversation, showing little or no interest in your life, experiences, or opinions?
- **Inconsistent Stories:** Does he tell you things that don't add up?
- **Keeping You in a Secret Compartment:** If he won't connect with you on social media, never invites you to his place, see you on holidays, or introduce you to his family and friends after a reasonable amount of time, there's a good chance he's leading a double life, which is your cue to exit.
- **Negative Attitude:** Is he a complainer, a hothead, or a pessimist?
- **Too Much, Too Soon:** Does he shower you with compliments and make grand, dramatic, romantic gestures or statements before he really knows you? Does he tell you about his sexual kinks before you've even kissed? Does he creep you out by reciting everything he read about you online?
- **Overstepping Physical Boundaries:** Does he get too up-close-and-personal before you've signaled you're comfortable with that level of proximity or contact? (Worse

yet, is he insistent on touching and crowding you even after you've signaled your discomfort?)

- **Excessive Drinking or Substance Use or Obvious Neglect of his Health**: No further explanation needed.

- **Saying He Doesn't Want a Relationship**: It doesn't matter how right for you he seems; if you're looking for a relationship, and he tells you this upfront, believe him and move on.

- **Playing the Widower or Divorcé Card Too Hard**: Does he make his belated or ex-wife a looming presence that takes over at times? Does he use that past relationship as an excuse for his emotional unavailability or high-maintenance behavior?

- **Financial Havoc**: Does he show signs that his finances are in turmoil, boast about his money, act like a cheapskate, or overspend to impress you? It's one thing to be in a good relationship, and stand by a man should he fall on hard times. Signing up for a nightmare is quite another.

- **Toxic Masculinity**: Does he regale you with stories about his fights and confrontations?

- **You have an uneasy "gut" feeling**: Trust your instincts.

The red flags you overlook early on are usually the same ones that will undo your relationship months or years later. If bright red flags keep popping up early on, grab your coat and skedaddle like you're escaping a lousy karaoke night!

Now, no matter how bad the date, fabulous Ladies don't feel compelled to regale friends, family, social media groups, or the next guy with dating war stories. It's just plain tacky. Remember the *Golden Rule*.

Avoid Getting Input from Well-Meaning Friends and Family too soon.
After a great date or two, your peanut gallery of well-meaning friends, family, and colleagues is often eager to crown a man "perfect for you"—particularly if he has a little charm or success. It's like they've stumbled upon something that sort of shines like a diamond and can't help but shout, "He's the one!" But a flashy photo, high status, or a shared interest does not a prince charming make. True compatibility takes more, and getting to know a man well takes time.

On the flip side, if you tell the people in your life about a misstep your new guy made on an early date, they may be too eager to sound the alarms and advise you to cut him loose. Suppose you later reconsider or uncover mitigating circumstances that explain his behavior? Once you have already spilled the tea, the damage is done, and his reputation will forever be tarnished in their eyes.

When it comes to finding a life partner, we have to sift through a lot of glitter to find genuine gold. So, play your cards close to the vest, trust your instincts, and remember, this time around, *you're* the one calling the shots when choosing a man.

Don't kiss and tell.

Treat the details of your intimate moments with the discretion of a secret agent—because who doesn't love a bit of mystery and intrigue? It's not just good for your reputation; it's downright sexy. After all, what elegant woman wants to broadcast her business?

Say "No" with Style and a Smile.

You're more attractive and desirable than you may realize. Now that you're suddenly single and back on the market, you may be surprised by the number of men who show interest in you. You can't date, sleep with, or commit to all of them, and elegant Ladies don't use dating for free dinners, gifts, or entertainment. If a man is interested in you and you can't reciprocate his feelings, you have a responsibility to let him down gently, *pronto*. If you can, do so in a way that gives him an easy, face-saving retreat. You may have to gently break a few hearts, but there's no need to crush any souls.

Remember: Silver Dating has a Silver Lining. Mature dating tends to be more authentic. We're more settled and more aware of what we want.

Exercise 16: Return to Romance

What kind of relationship are you looking for? Some women want romance and passion. Some want companionship. Some want a reliable, presentable date to take to social events. Other women are intent on remarrying. It's best to think about why you want to date and what you're really looking for before you start dating because, as the old saying goes, if you don't know where you're going, you'll probably end up somewhere else.

Here are some questions to ask yourself:

- Am I emotionally ready to start dating again? (In other words, have I fully processed the end of my marriage or partnership?)
- How would I want a new relationship to differ from my past one?
- What mistakes did I make in past relationship(s) that I can avoid this time? In other words, how can I be a better partner this time around?
- What qualities do I need in a partner?
- What are my non-negotiables in a relationship?
- What boundaries do I need in dating, and do I feel secure enough to communicate them effectively?
- What are my short-term and long-term goals for dating?
- How much time do I want to spend dating?
- Am I emotionally ready to cope with rejection?

Embrace this new chapter with confidence because your next great love story may be waiting to be written!

23

The Questionable Ethics of "The Friend Zone"

Gather 'round ladies, let's dish about the "Friend Zone." That term got tossed around on some T.V. show ages ago, and in the course of my life, I've seen my fair share of men trying to cozy up to it.

But guess what? They didn't end up there because I put them there. Oh no, they parked themselves in that spot by pretending to be my platonic buddy while secretly nursing a crush—only to vanish or get bent out of shape when I started dating someone else. Or they left me flabbergasted by a startlingly sudden sexual proposition or declaration of love.

We women, too, sometimes hang around male friends, quietly crushing all the while.

First off, let's call the "Friend Zone" what it is: dishonest. It's not cool for any guy or gal to play the buddy card while secretly pining for more, hanging out, feigning innocence, and then getting upset when things don't go their way.

We're no longer teenagers, so it's time to cut the crap. If you've got feelings for a male friend, spill the beans and risk getting shot down. If you don't have the courage to do that, quietly fade away from him and look for someone else.

And Ladies, if a straight man is spending way too much time with you, guess what? He's into you. Treat that elephant in the room with empathy and kindness, and if you can't reciprocate his feelings, give him an easy out so he can move on with his dignity intact.

Let every man in your life know where he stands. And Ladies, if you need a mechanic, a mover, a computer tech, a therapist, an ATM, or any other services, put on your big girl stilettos and handle it yourself instead of taking advantage of a man who hopes to win your heart.

So, go out there, be honest, be kind, and remember—Life's too short to deal with the Friend Zone in either direction.

24

You Found Someone You Like

"A heart that loves is always young."
—GREEK PROVERB

lright, let's explore that undeniable chemistry. One date leads to another, and suddenly, he's all you can think about. If he's a great guy, that's fantastic. But before you start picking out china patterns and naming your future pets, remember that times and men have changed. We may have been carefree about boundaries in our younger days—we may have even thought a parade of red flags made a guy seem all the more exciting. This time around, we need to watch out for ourselves more carefully by drawing some lines in the sand.

Men enjoy connections with women, whether or not they're falling in love. Sometimes, so much that it's easy for us to mistake their attention for affection—especially when we're feeling lonely; that's why we can't let our hearts run away faster than a dog off its leash.

Stay grounded in reality and give yourself ample time to see the relationship for what it really is. Getting too emotionally invested too soon tends to scare off a good men and attract a bad ones.

Women and men often see dating differently. Just because a man wants to date you doesn't mean he wants a real relationship. Men and women frequently have different views on sex, too. A lot of men see it as nothing more than entertainment with a physical release—like going to the gym, but with fewer clothes and more fun. So, please don't assume that sleeping with him will automatically lead to something more.

Building a relationship isn't a sprint. It's a marathon with a few hurdles. In the early days, it's wise to get to know each other at a safe and reasonable speed and to pay more attention to a man's actions than his words.

But by the same token, take whatever a man says at face value. Avoid reading between the lines like you're deciphering a cryptic crossword puzzle. If he says he's not looking for commitment, that's precisely what he means.

Manage your own emotions.

When you're wild about someone, it's like Cupid's taser has zapped you—the thought of them, a text from them, the sound of their voice, and any encounter floods your brain with oxytocin and dopamine. It's a love cocktail that makes you feel like you're floating on a cloud. And then, when you're apart, it can feel like you crashed back to Earth with a thud. Recognize this cycle for what it is, Ladies, and don't let that dramatic drop in "feel good" hormones turn you into a clingy emotional wreck. Your sanity is an excellent reason to pace the relationship slowly.

Avoid the Texting Dopamine Loop.

We all get a dopamine hit when we receive a text from a man we like, and that feeling is more addictive than clearance sale shopping. If your communication patterns keep you constantly glancing at your phone, you need to break out of that loop.

Whenever you're itching to text him, stop and ask yourself if the message is about genuine communication or emotional reassurance. Are you trying to find some "magic bullet text" because you're not satisfied with the current level of communication? When you scroll through your texts, are you sending paragraphs and getting back two-word answers? Trust me, Ladies, no man is worth straining your thumbs over.

Here's the bottom line. If you feel like a lottery winner when your phone dings and like you just lost your job when it doesn't, it's time to step away from his digital sweet nothings and reclaim your mental and emotional health. The best way is to respond to his next text with a straightforward message: > Call me. I want to hear your voice. ;) And let it go at that.

You Gotta Have "The Talk."

It might feel awkward to bring up how you feel about monogamy and safe sex, but if you're calling this a relationship yet don't feel you can express your needs, it's time to take a step back and figure out why.

Is this a real romantic relationship, or a vague situationship in which you have no idea what the Hell is going on? If you're unsure where you stand, you have to bring it up.

The right man won't run for the hills or start talking in riddles when you need clarity. Keeping quiet about your needs won't make the wrong man like you any better; it will just give him implicit permission to keep doing whatever he wants.

If you're about to cross the threshold into sexual intimacy and want an exclusive relationship, you'll have to go in with a "This is what I need, take it or leave it" approach and be fully prepared to walk if you can't see eye-to-eye.

Even if you're both okay with a non-exclusive arrangement, you'll still need to discuss ground rules and boundaries.

If you've been together and exclusive for a while, you may be thinking long-term, but don't assume he's on the same page. At some point, you'll have to ask, "If things keep progressing between us, what are your hopes for the future?"

Insist on Safe Sex.

Just because we can't get pregnant anymore doesn't mean the coast is clear. S.T.D. testing and safe sex practices aren't exactly the stuff of romance novels, but while we're single, we have to protect ourselves.

If you don't want to hold off on sex until you feel confident in a relationship and then both get tested, you'll have to break out the condoms. Sure, it's not the most fun or sexy topic, but neither are S.T.D.s, and by the way, they're on the rise in our older demographic.

So, when you're having "The Talk," you've got to lay it all out on the table. While you're at it, it may be a good idea to discuss your personal desires and fantasies to make sure you're compatible.

Oh, and by the way, when was the last time you read a serious book about sexual pleasure? If you can't remember when, get thee to a bookstore!

Your First Night Together

When it comes to intimacy with a man, feeling secure is vital for us women. Once you're ready to take that step, it's time to let go of any inhibitions. Fantasize about him beforehand to get into the right mindset. If you're worried about lubricating, find a product that helps. Likewise, don't be stunned or say anything if he uses a "little blue pill" to perform. Our bodies change as we go through life, but in romantic moments, the less said about it, the better.

Likewise, whatever you do, don't apologize for anything or make any negative comments about your body. You totally turned on—not faking—is the sexiest thing in the world to a man.

Dim the lights, slip into some gorgeous lingerie, and have fun. Whisper your desires to him and ask him what he likes. No matter how skilled or attractive he is, you'll probably need to take some responsibility for your pleasure. If he's not getting you there, gently guide him instead of responding with theatrics. Faking orgasm is an intimacy killer and a guarantee you'll get repeat performances that don't do much for you night after night. You'll start to resent him for your sexual boredom, even though it's arguably more your fault than his.

Be prepared that sex may bring out a side of him you haven't seen before. If he suddenly acts like he's driven by a motor, and you feel like you're in a lousy porn performance with a stranger who has no regard for your safety, comfort, or enjoyment, flip on the lights, and insist on a conversation. You'll either resolve things or uncover a dealbreaker neither of you had expected.

The next morning, be upbeat and don't give him any reason to think you plan to hang out all day. Have somewhere to be and something to do. Whether you know it or not, you both could use a little breathing room and processing time when the relationship is still new.

If you suddenly feel anxious after that first night, take a deep breath and hit the "pause" button on your worries. Assuming you did your homework, vetted the man carefully, and got to know him well before jumping into bed, most likely, everything's fine.

You two are an Item!

Remember, no matter how amazing this man may seem, he's not a superhero or a fantasy. No one person can make up for all of your past trials and tribulations or fulfill all of your dreams. Putting your guy on a pedestal is like expecting him to leap tall building in a single bound and catch speeding bullets in mid-air. It's not going to happen, and in time, it'll ruin your relationship.

Even the man of your dreams won't always get everything right—sometimes, the well-meaning things he says might be as misguided as using a fork to eat soup. Never forget, it's the thought that counts. So if he surprises you with ringside tickets to a hockey game, and you've never been a fan, appreciate his effort and the value of the tickets, and go with an open mind. You might just love it. You might not care to go again. Either way, it'll be a learning experience for both of you. Expect the early stages of a romance and getting to know each other to involve a lot of trial and error. Embrace this extraordinary time in your relationship and have fun!

25

Trouble in Paradise

*"Going out with a jerky guy is kind of like having
a piece of food caught in your teeth.
All your friends notice it before you do."*
—LIVIA SQUIRE

Let's get brutally honest. Are you seeing a man you find yourself making excuses for? Maybe even telling little fibs to make your relationship sound like a rom-com instead of the tragic farce it really is? It's easy to project qualities onto a man we wish he had, even if he hasn't shown them in real life. Are you exaggerating the intimacy or connection to your friends and family? Calling those late-night booty calls "dates" to save face? Giving him credit for emotional support he's about as capable of providing as a houseplant? And let's not forget, his "liking" your social media posts doesn't count as communication.

Ladies, let's not sugarcoat it. Denial is a robust defense mechanism, but believing and spreading flattering half-truths about your relationship won't turn Mr. Bare Minimum or Mr. Havoc into Mr. Right. And you deserve someone who recognizes your worth without you having to spell it out for him.

Men who treat women like pawns in their own game tend to be great at flattery, romantic gestures, and not much else. If you want something long-term, you need a man who enjoys your company in everyday moments. Does he invite you grocery shopping? Does he suggest you bring your laptop to his place and work from there? If he's not showing a preference for having you around when it's not all playtime and pillow talk, you need to find out why you're not connecting with him on a more meaningful level.

Too many otherwise intelligent women bestow W.I.F.E. (Washing, Intercourse, Food, Errands) benefits on men who haven't even committed to exclusive dating. These Ladies think proving to him how great they'll be in a long-term relationship will sell him on the idea. Sadly, all it does is make things worse. To paraphrase Picasso: Be a Goddess, not a doormat.

So you slept with a guy and now wish you hadn't?
A lot of women have done something a little out of character at one time or another. Granted, the aftermath of an offbeat interlude can be awkward. There's no need to say anything rude or hurtful. There's no point sticking around, trying to convince ourselves it wasn't a mistake either. Be ladylike, make an exit, and for the love of Aphrodite, get an S.T.D. test. Then, chalk it up to experience and move on. The less said about it, the better.

Breadcrumbing, Pocketing, and Situationships

Let's have a heart-to-heart about those relationships stuck in neutral.

Too often, women take too little responsibility for their emotional well-being by not asking the man they're seeing enough up-front questions and not getting enough straight answers while quietly curating an impressive collection of red flags. This usually happens because the woman really likes the man and figures if she's agreeable, he'll be more inclined to reciprocate her feelings. Huge mistake!

If you're involved with a man who won't move forward but keeps giving you little bits of encouragement because he doesn't want to let you go, he's a classic breadcrumber. Lace up your Doc Martens and kick that entanglement to the curb. It doesn't matter if he's afraid of his feelings, keeping you as a backup plan, or simply loves the attention. The outcome for you will be a big zero at best.

Most breadcrumbers, regardless of age, are as selfish and immature as a toddler with a toy truck. They know their "hot and cold" behavior is wreaking havoc on your heart, and they don't care.

When we were younger, we could be patient with immature nonsense, entertain a man's potential, and hope he'd grow up, but by this stage in the game, potential just doesn't cut it.

Today's dating app culture encourages men to be wishy-washy because they get hung up on the endless parade of swipe-worthy profiles. Their fear of missing out makes them frustratingly noncommittal. But let's be honest, Ladies. It takes two to tango when you're stuck in relationship Limbo. Your part? Going along with it while staying in denial. It's sort of like pretending Fudge Brownie Delight Sundaes don't have any calories and later blaming the scale.

On a related subject, if you've been seeing each other for a few months and he's avoided introducing you to his circle or meeting yours, you're being pocketed—and odds are, he'll never tell you the real reason for his secrecy.

Breadcrumbing and pocketing are signs you're in a situationship—in other words, you're being intimate, yet you have no idea about the terms of the relationship or where it stands. He may keep disappearing and then popping up with a flurry of texts, only to fade away again.

And it's not just about the sex. Men love affirmation and attention from women, too. Many of them will flirt and string you along to feed their egos and keep you around.

Any man who really likes and respects you will care about your opinion of him. If his behavior drives you to the point where you find yourself playing amateur detective or amateur psychologist, he doesn't like you very much. Demand respect, Ladies, and don't settle for less. If you allow mistreatment, you'll start believing there's something wrong with you, and we can't have that.

My Cautionary New York Tale

Since it's just us girls, let me spill the tea on a foolish move that wasted a year of my mature dating life. Learn from my blunders and save yourself the drama.

Picture this: I was in N.Y.C. rehearsing a play when a guy started messaging me on Nextdoor. He wasn't exactly Brad Pitt, and his persistence was a bit much, but he was witty. This went on for a couple of weeks. It turns out he was a diplomat and invited me to an embassy reception.

Mistake #1: I let him get comfy texting instead of calling. Spoiler alert: I probably got more than a few "copy/paste" texts.

Had I insisted on a better standard of communication from the get-go, he'd have either risen to the occasion or vanished.

We went to the embassy, and he suggested I plan the next date. I did. We went out the following Sunday afternoon, and neither of us could let that day end. We ended up at his apartment, talked all night, and I slept in his guest room—what should've been a three-hour date turned into a 19-hour conversation.

Mistake #2: By going to his place on the second date, even platonically, and engaging in an endless discussion, I made myself too available. Total mystique killer. Plus, it set unrealistic expectations for future dates and blurred boundaries way too soon.

Mistake #3: He was super intense about pursuing me in a way that led me to believe we had something special. We became intimate after just a few dates. Did we have "the talk?" Nope. Did we agree on anything? Nope. I was in La-La Land, liking him too much to force the issue. Wrong, wrong, wrong.

Mistake #4: My play opened, and he never came to a performance, dropped by the stage door afterward, or accepted an invitation to join me and the cast for after-show drinks—bright red flags.

Before I knew it, I was in an entanglement that was going nowhere. Yet I hung on, thinking I could turn things around and recapture the dynamic of those first few dates. After all, he was constantly texting, often flirty and romantic, and we had fun when we saw each other. Granted, he was a dud when it came to planning dates. Meeting each other's friends or family was apparently forbidden. Plus, he had a black belt in dodging direct questions.

So, what's the verdict? I let myself get breadcrumbed into a situationship in Limbo Land—and pocketed like a cheap accessory to boot! Partly, I'll admit, because I was overly impressed by his high-status job with all the bells and whistles, not out of opportunism, but out of fascination with his intellect. Not to mention that his fab foreign accent didn't hurt. When we're convinced a guy is a rare find, we tend to stick around. So, while I was bedazzled by this decorated peacock, I was turning down dates with quality men.

They say the definition of insanity is doing the same thing over and over and expecting different results, and boy, was I living proof! Ladies, if a smart cookie like me can screw up like that, anyone can. It's partly how our brains are wired—the sex, sweet talk, and texts trigger oxytocin and dopamine in our brains. These "feel good" hormones make us bond to a man. We hang on for the next "fix" while lying to ourselves that the situation will improve the next time we see him.

It doesn't help that a good number of men today, especially those in midlife, are riding high on the delusion that they'll always be catnip to the Ladies. This type of man plays games because, in the short term, he can. Some of them think juggling multiple women validates their status and success. Others are hedging their bets, hoping "Ms. Perfect" will waltz into their life and sweep them off their feet while keeping "Ms. Right Now" around as a bed warmer. No matter how you slice it, it's a no-win situation.

So keep your hearts in check, and if you find yourself making mistakes that even remotely resemble the ones I made, insist on a no-nonsense talk about values and expectations. If he responds by acting dodgy, walk away and don't look back. A man who has feelings for you won't risk losing you.

Ladies, let's be honest. We've got friends and, hopefully, some family, too. We can take care of ourselves just fine. All we need from a man are romance, intimacy, and the fun of partnership. Why waste time on a middle-aged man who pretends to be clueless so he can keep playing the field?

Know the value that you bring to a relationship.
Whether you're financially solvent or not, your female intuition is invaluable. We Ladies have a knack for knowing if our man's new business partner is a snake oil salesman, what his daughter wants most for her birthday, or whether he should pass up or buy that piece of real estate.

Men who are in tune with their masculine energy know that when their woman shares an intuitive thought, it's pure gold. But men who value women for traditionally masculine qualities—money, status, and being quick to jump into bed—are as clueless as a goldfish in a desert. They don't understand a good woman's true value in their life and never will. If the man you're seeing wants you to be someone you're not, he's not the man for you.

If You Break Up, Forget About Him.
If you break up, forget about him. Whether he told you he wasn't ready for a relationship and then married the next woman faster than you can say, "rebound," pulled a Houdini and vanished, or you tossed him out like yesterday's leftovers—just Let. It. Go.

If you keep renting space in your heart and mind to Mr. Adios Amigo, you won't have room for Mr. Happily Ever After. So delete his number, disconnect from him on social media, and move forward like the elegant catch you are.

One exception proves the rule above.

If someone leaves or rejects you, before you part ways, ask, "Why?"—assuming you actually want to know the answer. He might clam up or deflect, but if he spills the beans, hear him out with an open mind. If making a few minor adjustments can make your next relationship smoother without compromising who you are, it's certainly worth considering.

One last little secret about men

When you're feeling discouraged by these bewildering creatures called "men," remember, you don't need to understand them all. You only need to understand one—the man you end up with.

Remember: "It's better to be single with a standard than losing yourself for approval."—Unknown

IV

Zoom Along!

If you ever had a flat tire, you know you can't get far on a lopsided wheel. Your life is the same way. These diagrams aren't meant to illustrate that every area of life holds the same importance for everyone. The only point I'm making is that balance is essential.

Granted, there are seasons in our lives when something must be our top priority, but a huge imbalance isn't sustainable in the long run. We've all seen tragic stories of people whose lives were too far out of balance for too long.

Consider the wheels pictured on the following pages: one elaborate, two blank.

Reflect on your life today and fill out a blank wheel. (If you don't want to write in the book, trace a circle on a separate piece of paper.) For the sake of simplicity, divide the circle like a pie. Are there areas in your wheel that are over or under-inflated?

If so, it's time to think about making adjustments.

Next, fill out the second blank wheel with your better-balanced life, grab that metaphorical tire gauge, and get your Life Wheels balanced before you end up in a ditch!

Exercise 17: Zoom Along!

What does your present life wheel look like? Consider your Money & Security, Meaningful Work, Health, Spirituality, Home Environment, and so forth.

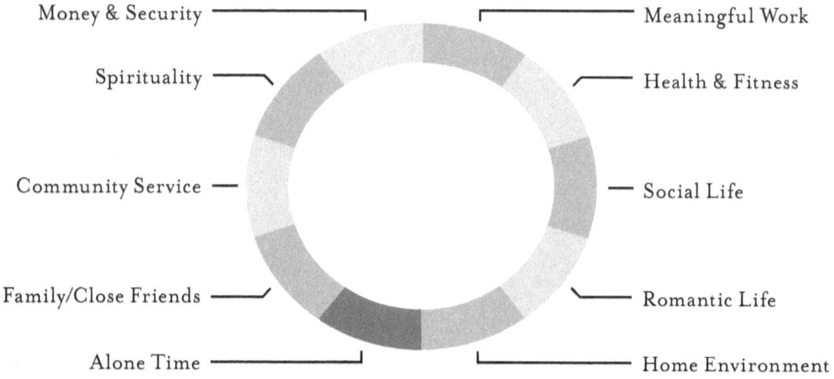

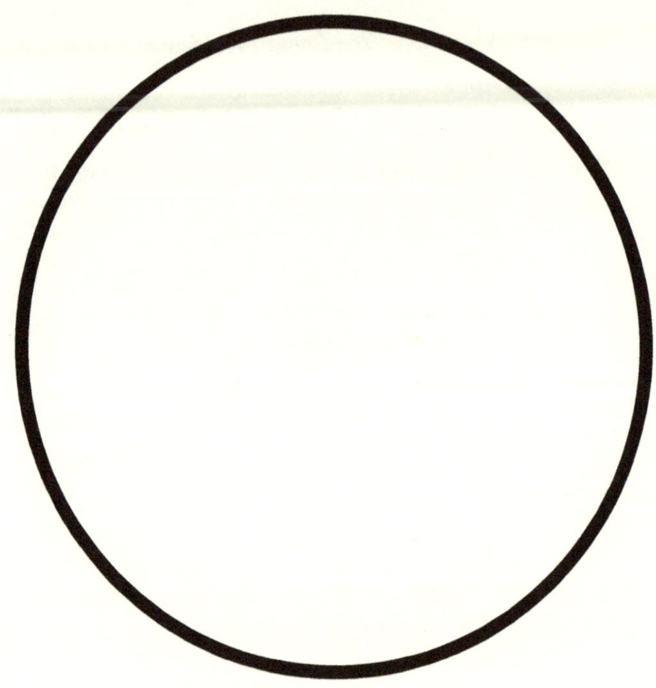

Look at the previous page or create your own categories. Divide the pie into categories that resemble your life today. Are you happy with it? If not, what changes can you make?

You're not likely to hit a target you can't see . . . so make it visual. What would your ideal life wheel look like?

What are the easiest, most sustainable things you can do to balance the wheel? It may take a few tries, but as you make progress, you'll find that every move toward balance makes your life run smoother.

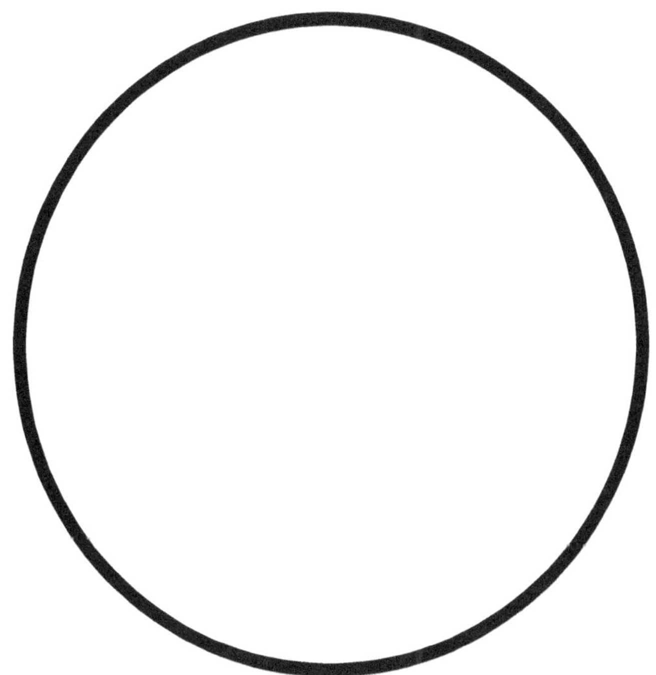

26

Your Remarkable Body

"Health and beauty aren't a goal. They're a lifestyle."
—Unknown

Ladies, let's get real: Health is Wealth, and it's up to us to make intelligent investments. Educate yourself, find trusted healthcare providers, and treat your body like the luxury vehicle it is. Because we're not just aiming for longevity; we're aiming for quality, vitality, and a fabulous life. So do your reading, make your appointments, ask questions, and embrace the power of taking responsibility for your well-being.

No Health Insurance?

Oh, Ladies, I've been there and learned some workarounds. First, scout out community clinics and medical schools that offer low-cost care. If you're job hunting, aim for one with benefits.

Got a minor health concern that's keeping you up at night? Consider looking into clinical trials. A quick *Google* search will reveal available options. Just remember, you might get a placebo, but hey, it might be worth a shot.

If you need a specific procedure, consider medical tourism. Some countries offer top-notch care at a fraction of the price, and if you travel a few days ahead of your medical appointments or stay until you're fully recovered, you can get a vacation out of it, too.

Keep your eye out for health fairs. Many offer free vision, hearing, blood pressure, cholesterol screenings, and more. And if your past includes a wandering ex, don't delay that STD test. Too shy to ask your doctor? The public health department's got your back with free or low-cost testing. Your peace of mind is worth its weight in gold.

For those lucky Ladies with stellar health, count your blessings and celebrate that gift. Treasure it like the crown jewel it is, and never take it for granted. Put your checkups, mammograms, colonoscopies, eye exams, dental visits, etc., on your calendar and show up. And don't forget those self-breast exams. At our age, I recommend getting a blood draw with your annual checkup. If you're low on iron, Vitamin D, or anything else, let your doctor recommend the right supplement. Extra calcium and a multivitamin may be good, but always check with your doctor. Remember, supplements aren't a substitute for a healthy diet.

You might also want to discuss hormone replacement therapy with a specialist. Some women swear by it, while others avoid it. Get the facts and make the best decision for you.

Reclaim Your Sexy Self

Let's face it, Ladies, by this stage in life, we've all been through the wringer—pregnancies, surgeries, and other physical challenges that don't exactly leave us feeling like supermodels. Many of us have also endured years of autopilot sex with men whose minds were elsewhere. But guess what? This is your chance to start over! For the first time in forever, no one's watching when you undress for bed or step out of the shower. That lack of pressure can be downright therapeutic as we get in tune with our physical side.

Once you're ready, grab a hand mirror and strip down in front of a full-length mirror. Look at your body from different angles—objectively—almost as if it belongs to someone else.

Focus on the good stuff. Maybe you've got stunning shoulders, lovely legs, a dazzling derriere, divine décolletage, Hollywood hair, a sparkling smile, etcetera. Own those assets and rock them.

As to the less than stellar . . . If you think I'm about to advise you to throw in the towel and blame it all on age or gravity, think again. Nobody picked up this book to be a wallflower. So let's get to work! A few small changes in habits and a lot of self-love can do wonders for your appearance and overall health.

Your Health and Beauty Journey Should Be Fun.
This isn't a crash course or a ten-week miracle. Sustainability is key. Now, I get it. If you're feeling Gung Ho, you might be tempted to swear off every drop of alcohol, caffeine, grain of sugar, and gram of fat and commit to waking up at dawn for a two-hour workout every day. But that's like trying to roller-skate on a tightrope—too easy to slip up big time. And guess what? After a slip-up, human nature kicks in, and we're all too quick to say, "Forget it!" and dive headfirst into an all-you-can-eat buffet.

Believe me, Ladies. I'm not here to preach perfection, and I'm not a health nut. If you want to learn about health, fitness, or nutrition in-depth, there are plenty of books, videos, and professionals out there. But no matter whose advice you choose, when it comes to your health journey, you're the captain of the ship. Don't just follow anyone else's map unthinkingly. Ask yourself, "Am I enjoying this, and can I keep it up long-term?" If the answer's "No," you need a new navigation plan.

You might be doing all you need to do already, but if you're huffing and puffing on a flight of stairs or feeling frustrated because you can no longer fit into half the clothes in your closet, it's time to make some changes.

A fitness trainer once told me that controlling our weight is roughly 75% diet and 25% exercise. In other words, no amount of exercise can outrun bad eating.

Fuel your body like the high-performance machine it is.
Even a little attention to your eating habits can make a lot of difference. Enjoy delicious meals. Embrace those vibrant veggies, lean proteins, flavorful fruits, and whole grains. Take small bites and eat slowly like royalty. When you eat out, remember those super-sized portions aren't a dare—split them and take half home. Being rolled out of the restaurant like a barrel isn't elegant enough for us, darlings.

Discover simple, healthy favorites you can whip up at home effortlessly; your taste buds—and bank account—will sing your praises. Before you go to a soirée, eat a bit to curb your appetite. Remember, you've been invited for your sparkling company, not to make sure all the canapés disappear!

Last but not least, remember the water. Two liters a day is the elixir of life, the magic potion that keeps you glowing. So, raise a glass of that water, toast to your fabulous self, and commit to becoming your healthiest ever!

Now, about food FOMO—let's not make diet-watching a drama, shall we? There's no need to walk past a French bakery as if you'll be facing a famine or the firing squad at dawn. Those delicious pastries will be there tomorrow, next week, and forever after that. Leaving them alone most of the time won't ultimately deprive you of anything.

As to alcohol, let's raise a glass with class. You're too fabulous to get saucy, embarrass yourself, and wake up with a headache the size of Texas. We want to toast to life, not regret it in the morning!

If you smoke or vape, it's like putting a velvet rope around your lungs and telling oxygen it's not on the guest list. Besides, nowadays, smoking limits your options. Non-smokers aren't always keen on dating smokers, and several studies have indicated that smokers have a more challenging time getting hired or earning top dollar. So kick the habit and open doors to a healthier, wealthier you!

Movement

Ladies, movement is magic—it pumps up those endorphins and kicks stress to the curb. Nothing works faster to make you feel younger and more radiant. So here's the deal: make exercise a non-negotiable part of your daily routine—no ifs, ands, or buts. Even if you're pressed for time and can't hit the gym or get out for a walk, you can always do something.

Now, if you're sitting there saying you "hate" exercise, you just haven't found the right fit yet. Trust me, there's something out there for everyone. So keep exploring until you discover an activity that sets your soul on fire. Let's face it: if we let ourselves become couch potatoes at our age, we'll start looking like potatoes in no time and end up underground like potatoes before our time! You may as well hang a "Do Not Disturb" sign on your fabulous future. So lace up those sneakers, find your groove, and get moving.

Whether you dance like no one's watching, power-walk like you're on a mission, stretch into yoga poses that make you feel zen, dink like dynamite on the pickleball court, or anything else you enjoy that keeps you in motion, your future self will thank you for it.

Mix it up! A healthy body needs strength, cardio, coordination, balance, and flexibility. Find activities you enjoy that cover these bases and find ways to incorporate them into your life.

Our body posture tends to turn inward as we age, but we don't have to let that happen. Think "expansion." Take deep breaths, stretch, and open your body posture. Remember the wise words of the Chinese: "You're only as old as your spine."

Along those same lines, fitness is an investment. As we move into our twilight years, we'll want to maintain our dignity by being able to handle simple things like getting to the toilet on our own. Build muscle now because you'll need it later.

Rest and Relaxation

You deserve to feel fabulous, not frazzled. At our age, more than before, we also need rest in addition to needing sleep. If you've been pushing yourself to the limit for years, it's time to listen to your body. Even a 15-minute power nap can make a big difference. Do what you can to schedule your life so that you don't feel exhausted too often. And no matter how driven or inspired you are, please don't schedule every second of your life! If you're chronically tired, sleepless, stressed, or feel like you have brain fog, your over-filled schedule may be part of the problem.

Window Dressing

Though our health, well-being, and inner beauty should always be front and center, let's consider the packaging. Here are my two cents—take them or leave them!

Update Your Wardrobe

This is a great time to give your style a little shake-up! Think of it as your personal fashion renaissance. Start by taking a good, hard look at your closet. If your wardrobe could talk, would it be screaming, "Help! I've been stuck in a time warp since the '90s!" or "Save me! I'm drowning in a sea of beige and bland?" It's time to give away those pieces that have seen better days or have been out of style for years. While you're at it, Ladies, retire those ratty old pajamas and lingerie. Embrace the glam—even in dreamland and underneath it all!

Before you hit the stores, study fashion magazines, blogs, and influencers. Look for a few good pieces that scream "you" with a contemporary twist. We're talking updated classics, bold accessories, and colors that make your skin glow like you've just had a week-long spa retreat.

Don't be afraid to experiment! Try that leopard print scarf, those funky earrings, or that sleek blazer. If you need help figuring out where to start, drag a stylish friend along or hire a personal shopper or fashion student for a day. And remember, this is about having fun and embracing your stunning self. So, twirl in that mirror, strut around your living room, and practice wearing your new look with confidence. You're not just updating your style—you're updating your attitude. Now go out there and show the world that you've still got it! In the words of legendary costume designer Edith Head, "You can have anything you want in life if you dress for it."

Update Your Hair

Your update wouldn't be complete without giving those lovely locks some attention.

Again, study blogs and magazines, then march to a good salon and chat with a stylist who gets you. Think of it as a hair therapy session. Whether you're going for a bold new change or something subtle, make sure it makes you feel like a superstar. If you have special hair challenges find a salon that specializes in the quality products and/or hair additions that will make you look your best.

To Gray or Not to Gray?

Gray hair is like any other accessory—it's all about whether you can rock it. Now, not all of us are blessed with the complexion, type of hair, or fashion flair to pull off that silver fox look—I tried it, and it did nothing but make me look frumpy and old.

While we were on the subject, a couple of years ago, an attractive neighbor my age went gray. One day, while we were both volunteering at an unfamiliar place, someone innocently asked if we were mother and daughter. Cue the awkward silence. The thing is, nothing about her looked a day older than me except her snowy locks. The question irked her, making the moment uncomfortable. But IMHO, sometimes, when we receive candid feedback—no matter how blunt—it's worth pausing and considering it instead of just shooting the messenger.

Now, I'm not here to tell you what to do with your hair color. But before you dive headfirst into the gray zone forever, make sure it's flattering and makes you feel terrific. If you try it and find it doesn't flatter you and make you feel great, consider it an experiment that didn't work and move on. We're aiming for fabulousness, not convenience or some misguided notion of integrity.

Update your makeup

If your makeup bag is a museum of products from the last decade, it's time for a major update. Start with a trip to your favorite beauty counter or store. Get a free makeover from a professional who can introduce you to the latest trends and products that enhance your natural beauty. Don't be shy about asking questions or trying new things. However, *do* be shy about dropping a fortune on that first visit. Consider your everyday lifestyle and how much makeup you really wear.

Great makeup starts with great skin, but good skincare doesn't need to cost a fortune. I use simple, inexpensive products you can find in a drugstore though to be fair, I inherited good skin.

If your skin is forever throwing a tantrum, talk to a pro. For all of us, consistency is key—clean, moisturize, and use the SPF level you need. And don't forget that diet, hydration, and circulation have just about everything to do with how healthy your skin looks.

Brows: If, like me, you no longer see well enough up close to shape your brows yourself, have them professionally done. Our brows can also thin out as we age, so fill them in with a brow pencil or powder that matches your natural color.

Overall skin tone: Opt for a lightweight foundation or a tinted moisturizer that gives you coverage without looking caky and settling into those fine lines. Look for formulas that are hydrating and contain SPF.

Eyes: I think for most of us, mascara is a must.

Lips: Keep your lips moisturized and choose stylish lip colors that brighten your complexion. And while we're looking at your mouth, nothing will detract from your smile like stained teeth. If your teeth look dingy, buy a home whitening product or have them whitened at the dentist.

No deferred maintenance allowed.

Grooming is all about routine, and the time for manicures, pedicures, hair coloring and trims, brow maintenance, depilation, etc., is before you look like you've been on a month-long camping trip. You're too fabulous to sport inch-long gray roots or nail polish so chipped it could double as abstract art. Let's face it: Shabby grooming speaks volumes about your self-esteem, cleanliness, and general awareness, and Murphy's Law dictates that the day you go out looking like an unmade bed will be when you run into everyone and their mother.

Turn Your Liabilities into Assets.

Of course, we all have beauty challenges. Style and confidence are the best ways to overcome them. For example, Jacqueline Kennedy had coarse, unruly hair. Instead of spending hours in front of the mirror trying to tame her tresses, she tied on a silk scarf and went about her day. This simple yet elegant accessory became a signature part of her look. Or think of the iconic Lauren Hutton—sultry and stylish with a gap between her two front teeth. Instead of going in for orthodontics or channeling the Mona Lisa, she smiled wide. That imperfect grin became one of her trademark features, which set her apart in the world of modeling and fashion. If you're dealing with a perceived flaw, you, too, can flip the script and make it part of your personal chic!

Nips and Tucks and Needles

In this age of "choose-your-own-adventure" in beauty, we've got a lot of options—Botox, fillers, lasers, you name it! If you're diving into the world of cosmetic procedures, you can find a wealth of information on *realself.com*—it's like *TripAdvisor* for your face and body, minus the vacation selfies. Just remember, while our culture jokes about cosmetic procedures, it's actual surgery with real risks and real pain and outcomes that can range from "Wow!" to "Oh no! What have I done?"

And please don't broadcast your cosmetic adventures. Sure, you can tell your inner circle—or even a passing stranger if you strike up a conversation and they tell you they're considering a little nip or tuck themselves. But front-paging it far and wide is a bit like a magician showing the audience how he hides the rabbit in his top hat before the show. It invites scrutiny and ruins the mystery. Besides, we never know what's being said behind our backs. You wouldn't want everyone looking at you through a different lens now, would you?

Stay Safe.

If there's one thing that can wear us out faster than trying to keep up with the latest *TikTok* dance craze, it's recovering from an accident. When we're flying solo, we simply can't afford to get sick or hurt—there's no backup crew. So, let's get savvy about dodging those unnecessary mishaps.

Safety isn't just about avoiding a trip to the ER; it's a top-tier beauty tip! Nothing ruins your glamour faster than a strained back, a swollen ankle, or a dozen stitches. So, let's talk safety and keep your remarkable body in one gorgeous, uninjured piece.

I can't say enough about avoiding an overall sedentary lifestyle. You're more susceptible to injuries if you're out of shape. So get up, stretch, dance around your living room like nobody's watching (because, assuming you live alone, they aren't), and keep that body moving!

In Addition

- If you live alone, consider setting up a daily text check-in with your bestie. It can just be a "thumbs up" or a "smiley face" emoji, but it's your little "Hey, I woke up, I'm still here, and I'm still fine and fabulous!" moment. These quick mutual texts not only keep you connected but also ensure you're both safe and sound. Think of it as your daily dose of security.

- Ensure at least one neighbor has your emergency contact info.
- Keep your health information and insurance cards tucked safely in your wallet—always!
- Stock up on essential first-aid items. You never know when a little TLC might be needed, and who wants to run to *7-Eleven* for a box of Band-Aids at midnight?
- Use your legs, not your back, when lifting, moving, and carrying anything heavy! *Google* can be your best friend when learning proper techniques. If you do heavy work regularly, consider getting a back support belt.
- Keep your floors dry and clutter-free. Toss those treacherous throw rugs, tidy up those unruly cords, and make sure those icy sidewalks are scraped and salted. The last thing we need at our age is a careless fall.
- Equip your home with life-saving smoke alarms, CO_2 detectors, a security system, and a trusty fire extinguisher—safety first is always in vogue.
- Avoid precarious activities when you're home alone. No climbing ladders or attempting risky feats—let's save those for another day when someone is with you.
- Wear closed shoes when doing heavy work or using power tools or sharp objects.
- Save your highest heels for special, mostly sedentary occasions.
- Dress for the weather, and heed those weather warnings and advisories.

- Always wear protective gear for sports—including a bike helmet.
- Never get behind the wheel buzzed, and always buckle up.
- Attend a self-defense class and get up to date on crime prevention.

Remember: Safety is the ultimate accessory to maintain your glamorous lifestyle.

27

Rethink and Revamp– a Fresh Start

"Freedom is the will to be responsible for ourselves."
—FRIEDRICH NIETZSCHE

Once you're ready to consider your future seriously, it's time to reevaluate your home from a fresh perspective.

Family Home: To Keep or Not to Keep.
That is the existential, mortgage-laden question. Some of us never had the option. Other Ladies get the house and either cling to it like a security blanket or eye the exit faster than you can say "property taxes." Whatever you do, don't let anyone pressure you into keeping a big, pricey house just for nostalgia or status.

Even if the mortgage is a distant memory, there's no medal for holding onto a house that's draining your bank account faster than a Vegas weekend. If your home feels more like a burden than a sanctuary, it's time to consider your options.

Now that your life has changed, your current place could morph from a cozy haven into a stale museum of memories. Downsizing could be the fresh start you need.

Forget keeping up with the Joneses—they've got their own drama to deal with. This is your moment to create a life that fits you like a bespoke suit. Plus, a move might just be the perfect setting for a new romance when you're ready.

If you keep your home, consider redecorating.

Creating a new sense of control over your environment may help you feel better mentally and emotionally. Redecorating will allow you to create a space that reflects your new chapter in life and feels like a true reflection of who you are now. Whether you're going for cozy and inviting or sleek and sophisticated, make it a place where you feel completely at ease and utterly fantastic. You're not just updating the decor; you're making a statement that this is your home, designed to suit your needs and preferences. So, grab those home decor magazines, start pinning like a *Pinterest* pro, and let your inner interior designer shine.

Your Grown Kids and the Family Home

If your grown kids object to you selling the family home, consider making it possible for them to buy it. Or look into hiring a property manager and renting it out until they can afford it. You could even rent it to one of them, but if you do, go through a property manager to ensure the landlord-tenant lines don't get blurred to your disadvantage.

If they still pressure you to keep the place but have no interest in owning or renting it, remind them whose life this is. You don't dictate where they live, so they don't get to decide for you.

Now's a great time to give them the family heirlooms they want and then sell what doesn't fit your fabulous new lifestyle, whether you move or not.

If your husband has passed away, offer his extraneous belongings to your kids, other family members, and his close friends before selling them or giving them away.

Paring down your possessions now will save your kids a major headache down the road. If they don't understand that, have them talk to someone who's had to clear out a family home after a parent moves into assisted living or passes away. Trust me, they'll get the picture!

So, slip into something comfy, declutter like a diva, and make this transition all about you.

If you downsize . . .

Let me dish out some truth: After my divorce, I moved and kept a ton of stuff in storage for a few years. In hindsight? Not my brightest move. Storage was a black hole in my wallet, and "out of sight, out of mind" was the harsh truth. When I finally got into that storage unit a few years later, I was surprised by how much of the stuff seemed like junk.

Moving is a beast, but once you're settled in a place that's a breeze to maintain, you'll love the extra time and cash.

Should you embrace your inner gypsy?

For the past five years, I've been living the dream, slow traveling a little, working online, and hopping from one fun furnished place to another with nothing more than a few suitcases. These days, most of us know some adventurous souls who've done the same thing in an RV, embracing their inner road warrior. Now, this nomadic lifestyle has its perks and pitfalls, and it requires serious planning and prep—think six months to a year—because there are a million little details to nail down. Even after you do, you'll still need to be ready to expect the unexpected and embrace the unknown.

I'm not here to tell you to pack up and hit the road or to stay put. I have no regrets, but I know I'll eventually want to put down roots again. So, whether you choose to embrace your inner gypsy or settle down, just make sure it's a choice that feels right for you.

28
Creativity

*"A rock pile ceases to be a rock pile the moment
a single man contemplates it,
bearing within him the image of a cathedral."*
—Antoine de Saint-Exupery, The Little Prince

Creativity isn't just for artists. Every single one of us has an imagination as lively as a puppy that's been cooped up indoors all day. It's bursting with energy, just waiting for you to open the door and let it run wild. If your imagination happens to be sleeping, all you have to do is wake it up. Your creative muscle is like any other. It needs regular workouts to make it agile and reliable. Even if you've never considered yourself particularly creative, believe me, you can be. In fact, it just might just be your secret superpower, waiting for the perfect moment to shine.

Our education system loves playing it safe, which is why we've all been taught to fear mistakes and stick to the tried-and-true. But Ladies, that's not where the magic happens. True brilliance lies in daring to be different. Once you give yourself the green light to unleash your creativity, oh, the places you'll go!

Remember when you were a kid, and someone handed you a piece of paper and some crayons? You dove right in, unworried, unapologetic, and unselfconscious. But as we grow older, many of us lose faith in our creative abilities. It's time to silence that self-doubt and embrace the brilliance of your original ideas. Yes, your creativity is valuable, and it's high time you recognize it.

Creative people don't dismiss any ideas that come to mind—even if they don't understand those ideas at first. So please, start valuing your ideas now! Be ready to capture inspiration, even if you don't know how you'll use it. As I mentioned before, I jot down ideas on index cards and keep them in a big envelope I call my "idea bank." Every so often, I sift through those cards, keep the gems, toss the stinkers, and give a little more attention to half-baked ideas that seem to have potential. This book was an idea that came to me in an airport five years ago, but even before that, it was a vague, half-baked phrase that sat in my "idea bank" for quite some time. The minute it came into focus, I started writing.

My oldest daughter, Gina, who created the cover and illustrations for this book, is a creative maven. Ever since she was little, she'd pick up random things and carry them home, explaining, "I can use that for something." Now, you may not want to take a broken alarm clock out of a garbage can or pick up dried cicada shells from the sidewalk, but please start collecting your ideas. Jot them down in a digital document or on paper, and if you see something that sparks an idea, take a photo of it. You're starting a new chapter in life; you need an arsenal of inspiration, and chances are, some of those ideas are seeds for accomplishments that will make you proud.

Setting aside a dedicated time and space for your creativity to bloom is crucial. Find a place where you can let your mind run wild without censorship. Strive to be prolific instead of perfect. I repeat: *Strive to be prolific instead of perfect.* You can always refine what you come up with later, but for now, just let your creative instincts lead the way.

Shaking things up and letting your creativity loose is the key to making your new life a vibrant tapestry of exciting possibilities. Best of all, the journey of creativity is as thrilling as the destination, and trust me, if you embark on this journey, you'll be in for the ride of your life!

Remember: "Imagination is more important than knowledge. For knowledge is limited to all we now know and understand, while Imagination embraces the entire world, and all there ever will be to know and understand."—Albert Einstein

Exercise 18: Creativity

Whether you're rediscovering your creative spark or igniting it in earnest for the first time, these exercises are designed to help you explore and enjoy your imagination. There is no "right" or "wrong" result. Just be yourself and let your imagination run wild.

1. Set aside 20 minutes. Write freely about anything that comes to mind. Don't worry about grammar or spelling—just let your thoughts flow. Later on, read through what you wrote and circle, highlight, or underline any ideas or themes that stand out. Could any of them be seeds for a creative project?

2. Choose a creative activity you enjoy or want to explore—drawing, writing, photography, theater, music, crafting, fashion design, dance, public speaking, etc. Join a class—online or in person, join a group, or simply commit to spending at least 2 hours each week on this activity for at least 30 days. Pay attention to what you learn about yourself and your creative potential.

3. Plan a solo outing to a museum, art gallery, theater, or concert—anything that interests you. Spend time observing and immersing yourself in the creative works. Bring a notebook or sketch pad, and jot any inspirations or ideas that arise during your visit.

4. Invite a few friends or family members to join you in a creative activity—painting, cooking, crafting, etc. Work together on a project, sharing ideas and techniques. Enjoy the process and focus on having fun and collaborating. After the activity, discuss what you enjoyed most about

the collaborative experience. How did working with others affect your creativity?

5. Get into the habit of doodling.
6. Find time for spontaneous play—whether with your grandkids, dog, classmates in an improv workshop, or anyone else. Rekindling your sense of playfulness will help you think on your feet more creatively.

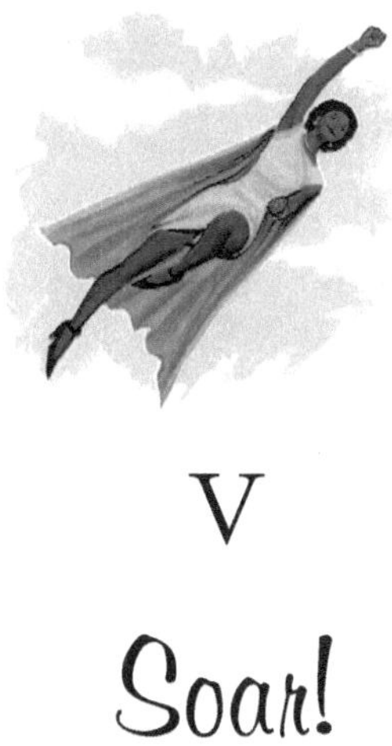

V

Soar!

I don't know about you, but I love the thrill of flight. I don't have a pilot's license, but I've been an eager passenger in everything from gliders and Cessnas to commercial planes of all sizes. Even if you don't like flying, stay with me while we look at the four forces of flight because they're a great metaphor for getting off the ground and soaring through life.

1. **Thrust:** The force that gets a plane zooming down the runway and into the sky. For us, it's the energy and momentum that propel us forward. This isn't just physical energy, Ladies; it's also inspiration and emotional oomph! Think about what fires you up like a rocket. Is it your dreams and goals? Your desire to change the world? Your kids and grandkids? Or something else? Whatever makes you want to spring out of bed and take the world by storm—that's your thrust. Harness it and charge forward!

2. **Lift:** This is the force that keeps a plane aloft. For us, lift is all about the "why" behind our goals and good habits that keeps us on track. Or to riff on the song, the wind beneath

our wings. Focus on what gives you lift and keeps you aiming higher.

3. **Drag**: Ah, that's the force that wants to pull us back and slow us down. But don't be fooled; drag isn't a villain. Sometimes, it's the wisdom that makes us pause and think twice before rushing headlong into a hot mess. Embrace drag; it's the grace and poise that ensure you make a grand entrance instead of a dramatic crash.

4. **Weight**: In flight, weight pulls the plane down and keeps it balanced and under control. Likewise, we need to shed unnecessary burdens and balance the responsibilities that are rightfully ours to carry. Once you get this right, you can rise with elegance and ease.

So, there you have it! Channel your inner aviator, find your thrust, embrace your lift, respect your drag, and balance your weight. It's time to take off and soar into that fabulous new life you've been dreaming of. Fasten your seatbelt and get ready for takeoff!

Exercise 19: Soar!

Think about the four forces of flight and how they apply to your life.

- Who and/or what pushes you forward?
- Who and/or what lifts you up?
- Who or what keeps you from diving headlong into things?
- Who and/or what keeps you stable?

If you read this book in order, you have collected and built some new tools and ideas to soar into the life you want.

This final portion of this book amounts to a calorie-free dessert. Let's dig in!

29
The Ageless Woman

"You can be gorgeous at thirty, charming at forty,
and irresistible for the rest of your life."
—Coco Chanel

If you're still clinging to the idea that age is a limitation, this chapter isn't for you, but if you're ready to embrace your ageless inner goddess, game on!

In the previous chapters, we covered mental, emotional, and physical well-being. By now, I hope you're starting to feel that instead of winding down, you're revving up for the adventure of a lifetime.

Becoming ageless isn't about trying to turn back the clock; it's about owning every inch of ourselves and feeling damn good about it. Sure, we were all dewy-eyed and line-free in our youth, but who wants to return to that naivety? We're wiser, stronger, and more interesting than ever before; if we work at it, we can keep improving.

So here's the deal: every morning, look in the mirror and tell yourself, "I am stunning and ageless!" Own those words. Embrace that concept. Let that confidence radiate from every pore. When someone compliments you on your good looks, smile and say, "Thank you," but let that compliment sink deep into your soul.

I know it's cliche, but it's also true. Every woman can be like a fine wine—better with age—but only if we choose to own it from the inside out.

Don't Talk Like a Fogy.

If you're given to generational griping, STOP! None of this "Millennials this" or "GenZ that" or "Young people blah blah blah" nonsense. That kind of talk will make you sound like an old crone and a cranky one at that.

Every generation has its shining qualities, so let's focus on the positives, shall we? Take a good look at the younger crowd and appreciate what they bring to the table. Instead of throwing shade, learn more about them. If you do, you'll find much to admire. Their music, blogs, humor, dances, and more are all part of their unique identity, just like ours was back in the day. And don't forget, they're the future. We should be cheering them on every step of the way!

Negativity isn't a good look on anyone, especially as we age. Stop griping in general—about your age, your health, the president, society's obsession with youth, etc. We're still sauntering about on this beautiful planet; we should be celebrating, not kvetching!

When it comes to your demeanor, remember this: ageless elegance is all about grace and class—on that note, there's no need to pepper your speech with vulgarity.

And nobody—I repeat, nobody—wants to hear every detail about your medical situation or your adventures in the bedroom. Save that stuff for your doctor or your memoirs. If every other woman in the room is chattering about her bowel movements or her penchant for nipple clamps, just smile like The Mona Lisa and preserve your lovely mystique. If they harass you about your silence, and a slightly playful "Wouldn't you like to know?" doesn't tone them down, you're with the wrong crowd.

And let's talk about nostalgia. It can be fun to reminisce, but a little goes a long way, so please don't get stuck in the past. Make it a point to stay current, and, for heaven's sake, don't be afraid to dive into new technology.

Remember, time is on our side when it comes to being the great equalizer. As we mature, style, taste, confidence, and experience can make all the difference. So what if we can't compete with the Instagram bikini babes? We had our days in the sun; those gals won't be young forever, either. Besides, if we could get that type of attention today, would we even want it?

While we're on the subject. . . no matter how slim and trim you are, if you're shopping at *Hot Topic* or raiding the Junior Department, you're not fooling anyone. You're telling the world you're desperately trying to cling to your youth. Nothing screams, "I'm older than I'm letting on," louder than in juvenile fashions on women of a certain age.

Your Secret Weapon

In addition to genetics and great health habits, there's another anti-aging secret I want to let you in on. Nobody talks about it, but I know it works.

The Power of Suggestion

As Buddha said, "What we think, we become." On that premise, crazy as it may sound, I've more or less convinced myself that I'm ageless—a bit like the portrait of Dorian Gray, but without the Devil involved. As the baseball legend Satchel Paige famously asked, "How old would you be if you didn't know how old you are?" Again, I'm not suggesting we run around in mini-skirts and frequent nightclubs with the college crowd, but we have to banish tired, dusty thinking and decide that, and even if we live to be 110, we'll never become that irrelevant old lady nobody looks at or listens to.

Age is linear, yet it's not a straight trajectory. It's more like a rollercoaster ride. When we're going through the wringer, we start to look older. A broken heart can leave us feeling and looking like we've aged a hundred years overnight. Yet miraculously, once the sun starts shining again—and it always does—we start looking and feeling younger again. Time may not fully heal all wounds, but it does a damned good job of patching them up. Every time life knocks us down, we can decide to pick ourselves back up again. There's nothing more age-defying than that.

And let's not forget the power of love. Falling head over heels can make us feel like we've found the fountain of youth in someone else's arms.

Use affirmations like:

- I'm dynamic and ageless.
- I'm healthy and energetic.
- I'm confident and charismatic.
- I'm an interesting woman.

If those affirmations don't feel honest, preface them with the words, "Every day I'm in the process of becoming more___________."

Remember: Not all flowers in the garden bloom simultaneously.

30

Timeless Elegance

*"Nothing makes a woman more beautiful than
the belief that she is beautiful."*
—Sophia Loren

Nowadays, everyone has more freedom than ever to rock whatever image tickles their fancy. We can wear our pajamas in public, flaunt the bedhead look in a Michelin restaurant, and spice up every sentence with an "F-Bomb." Nothing wrong with those choices . . . unless you want to be elegant.

Having polish and panache isn't just about vanity; it's about stacking the deck in our favor and playing the game smart. Looking the part and carrying yourself well is half the battle when it comes to first impressions in both the professional world and romance—areas where you want to take home first prize instead of a participant trophy.

When you break it down, elegance isn't about money; it's

about sensibility. Some millionaires don't know the meaning of manners and grace, while plenty of people with humble means exude natural charm and impeccable style.

At the end of the day, people all do the same basic things. We eat, sleep, communicate, occupy dwellings, clothe ourselves, bathe, make love, bear children and raise them, work, and so on.

What sets elegant people apart is *how* they do those things. And, might I add, as Yves Saint Laurent aptly put it, "We must never confuse elegance with snobbery."

Women of character aren't snobs; we're civilized forces to be reckoned with.

On that note, if you're looking for me to commiserate with you about women of a certain age being invisible, you've come to the wrong place. Ladies, if you've spent decades blending into the background, it's time to flip the script! Your life's not some B-list movie where you're just an extra. You're the leading lady in your blockbuster; if you haven't embraced that role, it's time to start. Your new life's not worth a dime if you never have a moment to own the spotlight. So, toss aside those old scripts of self-doubt and insecurity. It's showtime, darling!

Below is a list of elegant attributes. I'm not saying I embody all of these traits. I'm only saying I'm trying. I hope you, too, can use it for inspiration when you envision your fabulous future self. Remember, life is a chic adventure, not a perfectly polished destination!

A timeless, elegant woman is . . .

- Self-aware but not self-conscious.
- Confident in her worth, moral values, and beliefs but not so narrow-minded that she gets triggered when others express a different point of view.

- Current. She doesn't bother mentioning how attractive or sexy she used to be.
- Clean and well-kept.
- An embodiment of the phrase "Style never goes out of fashion!"
- Cool, calm, and collected because she's organized.
- Self-aware. For example, if she lives alone, every once in a while, she'll eat in front of a mirror to make sure her table manners haven't devolved into something that brings to mind a lumberjack putting wood into a chipper . . . and so on.
- Enthusiastic. Her zest for life shows in every little way.
- Warm, kind, thoughtful, and authentic. She appreciates people and makes them feel special.
- Aspiring. She knows she isn't perfect and never will be, but she always makes her best effort.
- Accepting. She doesn't see correcting others as her job. She can laugh at herself and admit to some of her faults unabashedly.
- Tasteful, calm, and confident.

Remember: Our time on earth is a bit of a survival contest. It's more fun for those who know how to survive with style!

31

Fascinating, Fun, and Fabulous

*"If you're in a comfort zone,
afraid to venture out,
remember that all winners were
at one time filled with doubt."*
—ANONYMOUS

The better you feel about yourself, the more exciting your life will become. Doors will open for you because you'll have the confidence to knock on them with the air of a woman who knows the secret password.

Here are some hints to make you even more fun, fascinating, and fabulous.

Develop a little star power.

Picture classic movie stars. You know those glamorous, larger-than-life icons who stole hearts and ignited imaginations worldwide. Back then, studios meticulously crafted their looks and style and even gave them exciting new names and backstories. But what made these stars truly shine? Their uniqueness. Each of those icons was a blazing comet of individuality. Ladies, if you want to harness some star power, you've got to follow suit. It's not about putting on a show; it's about rocking your authentic self.

Every woman is dull without a dash of pizzazz, so sprinkle some on! Whether it's your quirky style that makes you feel invincible, your knack for sending old-school postcards from vacations, or your talent for coordinating your dog's winter coat with your own, own it shamelessly. Maybe you're the Lady who serenades every friend with a heartfelt rendition of "Happy Birthday" on their voicemail. The possibilities to sizzle up your persona are endless. Remember, it's your show, and you're the star—so have a blast and shine bright. At this stage in the game, life's too short to play it small!

Cultivate the sexiest part of your body: your voice.

Ladies, let's discuss the magic of your voice. As we mature, the sultry depths of our vocal range can be mellow like smooth jazz, making even our laughter much more captivating than those high-pitched squeals. So remember, slow and velvety is the game plan here. And there's no need to holler when a whisper will do the trick.

And thank goodness for technology! Grab your smartphone and give your voice a spin. If it's not quite love at first sound, fear not. There are oodles of free online resources and apps to help you fine-tune your vocal finesse. Feeling extra fancy? Treat yourself to a class or voice coach—available for a variety of budgets, in-person or virtual.

Don't underestimate the power of your voice—I repeat, it's arguably the sexiest part of your body and a crucial part of your presence. Embrace it, refine it, and watch as it adds a splash of sophistication to your already fabulous self.

Harness the power of laughter.

As you navigate this wild and unpredictable chapter of your life, remember to find the belly laughs in the chaos. A woman who can chuckle at her predicaments is a powerhouse to be reckoned with. Make a point to sprinkle some humor into every day by reading or watching something amusing, and get into the habit of seeing the funny side of life.

Think of your wit as spice—too little is bland, but too much can be overwhelming. Jokes, funny stories, and witticisms ought to complement, not overshadow, your fabulous personality. Don't risk becoming the class clown whose punchlines too often fall flat. Last, don't kid around at anyone's expense. The person you're skewering may laugh along while resenting your every word.

Be a charming conversationalist.

Let's discuss the dying art of conversation. Needless to say, you should be worth talking to by keeping your life interesting, staying current, and having a few opinions. But here's the magic ingredient: LOVE.

Charming women walk into every social situation with genuine warmth and goodwill. They leave their competitive ego at the door. They ask thoughtful questions and really listen to the answers. They don't affect the stereotypical "active listening" body language because they know that nothing deliberate or presentational is needed when they're listening intently. They also know that people love being the star of the show without feeling like they're on trial or being forced to carry the full weight of the conversation.

Talking to people is a dance, not a monologue in either direction, so share your thoughts and vulnerabilities in an appropriate manner. Only ask questions you genuinely care about since phony baloney inquiries are easier to sniff out than cheap perfume.

Now, if you really want to earn your honorary doctorate in social charm, you can keep what used to be called a Farley File. These are notes on friends and acquaintances that you jot down alongside their contact information after each visit. Going that extra mile shows you care and keeps you ready for the next rendezvous with thoughtful talking points. Whether it's a grand gala or a cozy catch-up, remembering what people told you last time always goes over well.

Charm is a natural antidote to negativity and dullness. Last but not least, charm means knowing when to share the spotlight or graciously step aside—especially if there's a guest of honor.

Practice random acts of kindness.

There's real magic in everyday kindness. It's not about grudgingly handing a dollar to a panhandler without making eye contact—it's about having a genuine, compassionate heart and the desire to bring a little slice of heaven to someone's day.

Next time you're feeling a bit down, try this whimsical game. Raid the bank for a handful of half-dollar or one-dollar coins. Slip them into semi-hidden spots in public places, fairy godmother style. You'll never know who'll find them, but you can be sure each and every coin will bring a smile to a stranger's face and make them feel a bit lucky. Meanwhile, you'll feel like the magical Lady you are!

Be easy to please.

Other people have a need to make you happy, so make it easy for them. Let them know about your favorite little pleasures or quirky hobbies. Got a thing for exotic spices? Collect miniature elephants? Love lavender soap, tulips, or books of quotations? Work this information into natural conversation so your friends can hit the gift-giving bullseye without breaking the bank.

Never break character.

We humans excel at spotting patterns—it's a survival trait so we can identify our allies. Keep this in mind and stay true to your fabulous self because predictably awesome people make better friends than people who seem to wake up in a different world every day.

What's in a name?

At this turning point, you have the power to redefine yourself in any way you want. Some Ladies find it empowering to reclaim their maiden name or spice up their given name. If everyone calls you Kathy, but you feel more like a Kathleen, now's the time to go for it!

And as to the people you adore, why not toss a little nickname magic into some of those relationships? Pet names can add sparkle, warmth, and a whole lot of fun. Not that bland, patronizing "Honey" or "Sweetie" nonsense. But imagine, for example, calling your bestie "Sunshine" instead of plain old Sarah. Instantly, it's like you two have a little world where everything is just a bit more fun. So, get out there, call yourself and dear ones what you feel is best, and be the one-of-a-kind original you were born to be.

Be a Delver instead of a Dabbler.

When it comes to pursuits, there are two types of folks in this world: Dabblers and Delvers. Dabblers flit around from one thing to the next like butterflies in a cottage garden. In July, it's watercolor painting. In September, it's jujitsu, and by November, it's astronomy. They think their constant hopping around makes them interesting, but let's be honest—they're more than a bit ho-hum. Chat with a Dabbler, and there's not much going on beneath the surface.

Now, let's get to the Delvers. These folks have a passion so deep it could drill into China. Whether stargazing, strumming a banjo, or whipping up gourmet delights, they know their stuff and are darn good at it! Ask a Delver about their passion, and get ready to be dazzled by their knowledge and skill.

When you hear a eulogy, the deep interests get mentioned, not the flitting about. So, if you want to be memorable in life and ever after, find something you love and master it. By all means, try new things on the side—who doesn't love a little variety?—but remember, deep interests are the four-lane superhighway to becoming a woman of substance. Dabbling? That's just the cotton candy at the fair.

Become a bit of a raconteur.

Ever heard of a raconteur? They spin entertaining tales with charm and relevance—and let's face it, everyone loves a good story.

We all have stories waiting to be shared. Soak up life, observe keenly, and have a few good tales you can weave into conversations.

Just be yourself, stick to one story per gathering, keep it snappy, and please, no repeats.

Now, if you want to be a storyteller, practice is key. Read aloud, join Toastmasters, take an improv class, or just practice at home alone. Great storytellers engage their audience. They understand pacing and are not afraid to slip into character or add a twist for laughs.

I think every fabulous Lady should give storytelling a whirl— Who knows? You might just have everyone rolling with laughter!

Be thoughtful in small ways.

In general, sincere compliments, remembering names, small random gifts, and gracious gestures never go out of style. Neither does remembering someone's pain points and steering clear of them both in conversation and in tangible matters. And while a quick "Happy Birthday" on social media suffices for acquaintances, true friends deserve the royal treatment—a heartfelt phone call or a surprise floral delivery. Trust me, nothing says "I care" like old-school mail or flowers.

Be playful and spontaneous.

Attention Ladies, let's set the record straight: Elegance isn't about being stiff or formal. It's about radiating a lively spirit. Charismatic folks bring joie de vivre to every occasion because they're always ready to dive in and have a blast. Even if you're decked out in an evening gown, don't forget to loosen up and have fun!

Get into the Arena.

You can't master a skill in a vacuum; join leagues, clubs, tournaments, classes, open mic nights, and contests. Whatever will push you into friendly competition will connect you with like-minded folks and turbocharge your learning. As to the thrill of possible victory? That's just the icing on the cake! I think every fabulous Lady should occasionally dive into a competition in at least one area of her life and enjoy every moment of it!

Take some plunges.

Your best years are still ahead, Ladies, so be flexible enough to bend with whatever life throws at you. Jump into new experiences without overthinking. Take the letter "T" off the word "Can" and let the adventure begin!

Exercise 20: Fabulous You

If you're this far into the book, pat yourself on the back. You've been patient and persistent, unpacking the layers of your personality like a set of Ukrainian nesting dolls. It's finally time to take all that newfound self-awareness, sprinkle in some determination, and march forward with the confidence of a supermodel, the resilience of a drag queen, and the tenacity of a Broadway star. Get ready to step out like you own the stage because you do!

Envision the most fabulous future version of yourself possible.

- Where does she live?
- How does she dress?
- What does she do professionally?
- What is she good at?
- Who are the most important people in her life?
- How does she stay fit?
- When people ask her about her life, what does she say?
- Who does she date?
- How do her love interests treat her?
- How do people describe her?
- What is she passionate about?
- What are her goals?

Fix that ideal future self in your mind. Once you start using that version of yourself to make little, everyday choices, you'll start feeling more like your ideal. This concept isn't about play-acting. It's about gradual, sustainable change.

Study interviews of the women you admire most for inspiration. Make them your role models. Last but not least, remember the sky's the limit! Please don't get so set on what you want that you refuse to accept something even better when it comes along.

32

Chez Vous

"You can have more than one home.
You can carry your roots with you
and decide where they grow."
—HENNING MANKELL, SWEDISH WRITER

Your home? It's your kingdom, your sanctuary, your place where pants are optional. . .

Now, believe me, I know life isn't always a fairy tale. Sometimes, we lose everything—our homes, our comfort, and our sense of security. Going through that upheaval isn't easy, but it's survivable. Should you find yourself bouncing from place to place, feeling like a turtle without its shell, don't you dare feel ashamed. Get a PO Box or mail service, store what won't fit into a suitcase or two, hold your head high, make no apologies, and push through, embracing the adventure, believing you'll find your way back.

And whether you live in a rented room or mansion, make

your home as uniquely you as possible. Your space has vibes that hit everyone who enters right in the gut—including you. So, make it a pleasant feast for all five senses. Whether it's the aroma of good ol' coffee, a crock pot of soup simmering away, or your favorite natural cleaning products, you deserve a home that smells pleasant the minute you cross the threshold. Make it easy on the eyes, clean and uncluttered, and while you're at it, comfy as heck. Fill the air with music that suits your mood, nature's sweet serenade, or beautiful golden silence. The better your environment, the better your outlook, so don't shortchange yourself.

Moving to a new community?

Off to new horizons? Whether near or far, let's do it right, Ladies! First, do your best to make a great entrance. Move-ins are prone to causing a little chaos, so show up at a civilized hour looking presentable. Lugging suitcases or carrying boxes calls for casual, not sloppy, attire. After all, move-ins are filled with first impressions.

Don't expect a welcome wagon if you're headed to a big city. Urbanites value their privacy like it's gold, so don't feel snubbed if your new neighbors keep to themselves.

On the other hand, if you're venturing to a small town or the 'burbs, the welcome committee might swing by before you're done unpacking your boxes. Be prepared to stop and have a pleasant conversation; if they give you anything, accept it graciously.

It's best not to leave making friends in your new community to chance. Think about the kind of people you vibe with and attend meetups, activities, and hangouts where you'll likely find them. But take your time adding anyone to your inner circle. You might meet a terrific person who is having a bad day or someone who makes a lovely first impression but hides a problematic side.

Likewise, don't be in a hurry to show off your unique talents or talk about your accomplishments. Jumping the gun on those things telegraphs insecurity or competitiveness instead of mature confidence. And anyway, you're naturally likable, attractive, and well worth knowing, remember?

Moving Cross Country?

Dial up your curiosity to max—while adapting to your new locale's unique flair, fashion norms, and culture, and be prepared to say "Yes" to new food experiences. Brace yourself for a different climate, knowing you might swap old allergies for new ones. Learn about the local health risks, like Lyme disease in the Northeast or Valley Fever in the Southwest, and remember that not all air quality and tap water are created equal. Find out and filter if needed. Last but not least, if you're moving to a region with potential hurricanes, tornadoes, earthquakes, or wildfires, have a disaster plan in place.

Here's to new horizons and new opportunities!

33

Walk Naked

"Observation is the key to intelligence."
—HUGH LOVELL

I knew the title of this chapter would get your attention. But unless you're living off the grid or in a nudist colony, please don't take that advice literally. Though I want your journey to be full of adventures, let's not end up in the back of a police cruiser, shall we?

In this context, I'm talking about taking a walk with your mind "naked." That means no podcasts, no music, no audiobooks, and definitely no phone calls. Sure, bring your phone for emergencies, but keep it turned off and stashed away.

Thanks to the siren song of technology, our attention spans are shrinking faster than a Guernsey sweater in the dryer. Unplugged walks will help give your mind the downtime it needs for reflection, contemplation, and emotional processing. Your inner voice has wise and helpful thoughts, but you won't hear them if they're drowned out by constant din. However, it would be best if you didn't walk around like a zombie or ruminator. Here are some themes and prompts to enhance your Naked Walks. Feel free to come up with your own:

- **Selfless Stroll**: Devote your walk to thinking of someone else—ponder something you can do for them.
- **Observation Walk**: Stroll through a familiar place with the intention of noticing things you've overlooked countless times.
- **Walkie-Talkie Therapy**: That phrase was coined by my friend, Shelby, who credits these walks for the quality of her marriage. Take a close friend or loved one along and have a "heart-to-heart." Walking side by side without eye contact makes speaking openly and honestly easier.
- **Sentimental Stroll**: Walk in a place that holds a lot of memories. Recollect and feel the stirring of your own emotions. Give yourself time to understand what you're feeling and why.
- **Wisdom Walk**: Seek wisdom through observation. Maybe you'll overhear a pearl of wisdom or see something that makes you think of a wise metaphor. When you get back, make a point to write down and share your newfound wisdom.
- **Adventure Walk**: Explore a new, safe neighborhood or outdoor area. Don't go home until you've seen something surprising or amusing. Make a mental note to share the experience with someone later.
- **Feast for the Senses Walk**: Focus on sights, smells, textures and sounds. If something is captivating, stop and study it. Make mental notes and describe the experience later.

Exercise 21: Document Your Success

. . . It's not about how you start. It's about how you finish!

Remember the video diary you made at the beginning of this book? It's time to make another and compare them side by side.

Turn on your camera and answer these questions:
How have I changed my life since the beginning of this process?

- What obstacles did I overcome?
- What are my biggest accomplishments so far?
- What are my biggest dreams?

Compare both videos.

34
Final Thoughts

Thank you for joining me on this wild ride. After delving into your personality like a mystery novel and setting up your goals like targets on an archery range, you made it to graduation.

Now, graduation wasn't invented to tell us we know everything—it was invented to say, "Get out there and learn some more!"

On that note, I hope you've found some meaningful ways to better yourself and your life.

If you have a friend or loved one you think could benefit from this book, please share it or treat them to a fresh copy.

Last of all, I'd very much appreciate it if you went online and gave this book an honest review.

Forever Yours With Gratitude.

Caroline Sposto

Addendum

Poverty Among Older Divorced Women—Can We Promote Change?

High poverty rates among older widows get all the headlines, but guess what? Older divorced women are even more likely to be poor. And with divorce and remarriage trends, we're looking at a future where a larger share of retired women will be divorced.

Social Security laws have historically presented challenges for divorced women, and that's one reason older women are 80% more likely to be poor than older men.

Until 1948, everyone filed income taxes alone, regardless of marital status. Then, the policy changed to stop couples from "income shifting," where one high earner could put both into a lower tax bracket by splitting the income. These laws were written in an era when divorce was rare, more people owned homes, and ex-wives received alimony. Not to mention, those Social Security laws were also written by men.

Fast forward about 70 years to the 21st century, and we're still stuck with antiquated laws, opinions, and social norms that devastate women of our age group economically.

If your marriage lasted at least ten years, and your family responsibilities significantly impacted your lifelong earnings, you may not be eligible for much Social Security money on your own. However, you'll be entitled to Social Security benefits equal to up to 50% of your ex-husband's benefits. (For example, if he draws $4000 per month, you can draw up to $2000 per month. That $2000 doesn't come out of his income. It's separate. He'll still get the full $4000.) This provision is supposed to acknowledge that many of us spent decades in non-compensated roles, raising kids, supporting our husbands' careers, and often contributing our skills and sweat equity to a family business without official compensation. But it doesn't begin to account for all of the unpaid labor we provided—or the fact that, in many cases, it was the husband who willfully, and even maliciously, caused the demise of the marriage.

Granted, we can also receive survivor benefits if our ex passes away, and if we remarry after age 60, we can keep those survivor benefits. But let's face it, this arrangement still doesn't cut it. Women who had a series of marriages that fell slightly short of the 10-year mark or had long partnerships in states where common-law marriages aren't recognized are left high and dry.

To add insult to injury, our exes can remarry as many times as they wish and never lose a penny of their Social Security income. However, when we remarry, we lose our share of our ex-spousal benefits entirely. We can claim eligibility based on our new spouse's Social Security after one year. But if our new spouse is entitled to only a small amount of Social Security or is a foreign national with no Social Security benefits, we're out of luck.

Theoretically, we could live with our new partner instead of legally marrying him to keep our ex-spousal Social Security benefits, but why should any woman be put in that position?

And even if we were to remarry a man who has excellent Social Security benefits, if we end up divorced before the 10-year mark, again, we'll be out of luck.

Meanwhile, our ex-husbands can continue to draw twice as much money as we do, remarry as many times as they want, and never have to worry about losing their Social Security benefits.

Obviously, these laws need to be reformed. Ladies, I urge you to look into your Social Security benefits if you haven't already. See what they say, and if you find that you're in a dilemma, email your story to savvysurvival@icloud.com. I'm not sure what the next steps should be, but I do know that if we want to fight for change, we'll need to leverage the strength of numbers.

Here's to facing the future like the dynamos we are!

Look good, think straight, feel deeply, and communicate well.

Hugs!